At Issue

What Is the Impact of Emigration?

Other Books in the At Issue Series:

At Issue

What Is the Impact of Emigration?

Olivia Ferguson, Book Editor

GREENHAVEN PRESS
A part of Gale, Cengage Learning

GALE
CENGAGE Learning™

Detroit • New York • San Francisco • New Haven, Conn • Waterville, Maine • London

GALE
CENGAGE Learning™

Christine Nasso, *Publisher*
Elizabeth Des Chenes, *Managing Editor*

© 2011 Greenhaven Press, a part of Gale, Cengage Learning.

Gale and Greenhaven Press are registered trademarks used herein under license.

For more information, contact:
Greenhaven Press
27500 Drake Rd.
Farmington Hills, MI 48331-3535
Or you can visit our Internet site at gale.cengage.com

For product information and technology assistance, contact us at

Gale Customer Support, 1-800-877-4253
For permission to use material from this text or product, submit all requests online at www.cengage.com/permissions

Further permissions questions can be e-mailed to permissionrequest@cengage.com

Articles in Greenhaven Press anthologies are often edited for length to meet page requirements. In addition, original titles of these works are changed to clearly present the main thesis and to explicitly indicate the author's opinion. Every effort is made to ensure that Greenhaven Press accurately reflects the original intent of the authors. Every effort has been made to trace the owners of copyrighted material.

Cover Image copyright © Images.com/Corbis.

LIBRARY OF CONGRESS CATALOGING-IN-PUBLICATION DATA

What is the impact of emigration? / Olivia Ferguson, book editor.
   p. cm. -- (At issue)
   Includes bibliographical references and index.
   ISBN 978-0-7377-4695-2 (hardcover) -- ISBN 978-0-7377-4696-9 (pbk.)
   1. Emigration and immigration. I. Ferguson, Olivia.
   JV6035.W33 2010
   304.8--dc22

                                                           2010013957

Printed in the United States of America
1 2 3 4 5 6 7 14 13 12 11 10

Contents

Introduction

Currently in the emigration debate a new trend seems to be developing. Where America used to be the destination for many emigrants, a growing number of people are now leaving it behind. According to Mexico's National Survey of Employment and Occupation, around 433,000 Mexican emigrants returned home between February 2008 and February 2009, and slightly more than that the previous year. Mexico's central bank, Banco de Mexico, has also reported that remittances were down from $2.1 billion in April 2008 to $1.7 billion in April 2009. After speaking with several emigrants in Colorado, Associated Press writer Ivan Moreno found that while the economic downturn in America seems to be the primary cause for the reverse of the emigration trend, it is not the only reason.

Many emigrants are choosing to return to Mexico with their spouses who have been deported, like Vicenta Rodriguez Lopez, who says without her husband she can no longer afford to live in Colorado; however, her twenty-one-year-old son, who is in the United States illegally, plans on staying. Another, Roberto Espinoza, is heading back because after working as a mechanic for a General Motors dealership for eighteen years, he was denied a renewal on his work permit and did not want to stay in America illegally. Jesús Luna and his family who have lived in Colorado Springs for four years are heading back to Puebla to take care of his parents who are in poor health.

Then there are those who only come to the States long enough to make the money that they would need to live comfortably in Mexico. Gustavo Camacho has been to the United States twice. In 1999 he saved up enough money to go back to his home state of Jalisco and purchase a house. Since returning to the States in 2005 he has been able to save up enough to return to Jalisco and start a business of his own. He wants to be able to raise his six children in Jalisco because he feels that family values are stronger in Mexico. Some of the lesser reasons for returning to Mexico have been the crackdown on illegal immigration and anti-immigrant sentiment.

Another factor in this trend is the number of Americans that are leaving the United States for Mexico: Global relocation firms and recruiters confirm this, with the Mexican consulate in New York reporting an increase of almost 40 percent in the number of Americans inquiring about the requirements to relocate to Mexico. Louis Nevaer, the director of the financial services organization Hispanic Economics, notes in an article for New American Media titled "Many Americans Moving to Mexico in Search of the American Dream," that while Americans leaving for Mexico is no new phenomenon, it is the type of people relocating there that is. Where the majority of American emigrants to Mexico used to be retirees who could afford a higher standard of living there, professionals sent there on business or people trying to escape different situations in the States, such as alimony and child support, the new crop of emigrants are young people starting families and entrepreneurs.

One of the American emigrants that Nevaer spoke with, John Rogers, explained that "top of the list is that the economic benefits of being here allow us both to spend far more time with our son Johnny than we would be allowed if we lived the same style of life back in New York." He tells Nevaer that both he and his wife would have to work full time and their son would have to go to daycare and have a sitter at home. Also noted is that the community of Mérida, Mexico, is a very family-oriented place, welcoming families with babies and children. John and Nicole Larsen, another American couple, believe that the combination of language, culture, people, and customs will have a very positive effect on their young daughter. They are also a part of the group of entrepreneurs that have come to Mexico looking for better business opportunities.

Mexico is not the only place, however, that American emigrants are heading to, and these are not the only reasons. Other popular destinations include Europe, particularly Spain. Among other reasons that expatriates cite are affordable health care and their disgust with corruption in the United States government. People leaving America is one side of emigration that is often neglected by the media. The following viewpoints show that American emigrants have much in common with emigrants from other countries and their reason for leaving their homelands, which is generally to find a better life.

1

Emigration Damages Mexican Culture and Infrastructure

Norma Linda Ureña

Norma Linda Ureña is a lawyer in Seattle, Washington.

When the issue of immigration is debated, the focus is on the impact that it has on the United States. The effects that it has on the Latin American countries and their people are rarely, if ever, discussed. The biggest problem that emigration has created for Mexico is the loss of its young men, causing a rise in fatherless families and damaging Mexico's social infrastructure. This also leaves citizens vulnerable to foreign invasion, with not enough young men to defend their home country. The country's economy has also become dependent upon remittances from emigrants to modernize itself, and in this has failed to preserve much of its culture. The United States has taken advantage of this sacrifice, with no thought as to how Mexico may be affected, and only becomes concerned when immigration begins to influence its economy. Both countries must acknowledge what is happening in the Latin American countries and work together to find a solution to the problems that unrestrained immigration has created.

When you think of the problems associated with immigration, perhaps you think of Latin men standing on street corners asking for work, or maybe an image of families working in the fields comes to mind. But there is no doubt that mental pictures of Latinos illegally crossing the United States border are certain to fill your thoughts.

Norma Linda Ureña, "No Immigration Without Emigration: Consequences for the Countries Left Behind," *In Motion Magazine*, February 7, 2007. Copyright © 2007 NPC Productions. Reproduced by permission of the author.

Certainly you've read about the effects the recent and continuing wave of immigration is having—or is thought to be having—upon the United States. Of course, there is much impassioned debate whether the effects are good or bad. Clearly, arguments to support both sides can be made. Nevertheless, a large influx of laborers willing to work for any wage above $2 an hour arguably creates a wide range of consequences for U.S.-born workers. Some argue for the benefits of increased cultural diversity; others emphasize the burdens undocumented aliens place upon the social services of American towns, cities, and states. Some argue that the immigration of low-skilled, primarily Latino workers is valuable because it provides employers with a ready supply of labor to do the work that Americans consider to be undesirable and undercompensated; still others argue that the addition of such immigrants to the workforce will ultimately drive down the level of wages even in more desirable work situations. In any case, if you still find yourself undecided, there are plenty of talk shows, political debates, and newspaper articles dedicated to the analysis on both sides of the issue.

Throughout all this debate, little—if anything—is said about the effect on the Latin American countries people are leaving.

Emigration's Effect on Mexico

Interestingly enough, throughout all this debate, little—if anything—is said about the effect on the Latin American countries people are leaving to come to the United States. Take Mexico, for example. When my father left a small village in Jalisco in 1950, he was 20 years old and the oldest of six children. As the oldest son, he was also set to inherit the ejido (a communally owned Mexican farm) passed on to his father as a result of the Mexican Revolution in the 1900s. Instead, he had heard that he could make more money working in the fields for other people than harvesting sugarcane and corn from his own land. So, my father and two of his friends showed up at a gathering in Guadalajara. This gathering was set up at the request of U.S. farmers looking for braceros or manual laborers. Wages were minimum, but room and board were included, as well as transportation to and from the border. My father was chosen and he was told to report to the border town of Nogales. His first work assignment was in Stockton, California. He worked at this assignment for a few years and eventually earned the right to legal permanent-residency status. That was all in the years following World War II, when the United States needed hard-working men to replace those who had lost their lives in the war.

However, times in the United States are different now. Even though the United States is at war, there is no shortage of manual labor. Now, landowners—both farmers and ranchers—no longer need to cross the border to recruit workers to come here. Those workers who were wooed in the past with promises of room, board, and decent wages no longer need to be convinced. Today, workers freely come to the United States to work, crossing the border, leaving their families, and risking their lives.

Mexico in 1989

Eighteen years ago [in 1989,] I spent a summer in my father's village in Jalisco. I was in college then, and I have always had a strong and fond connection to the place. We used to spend our summers there when we were kids. I remember those days as if it were yesterday. The days seemed endless. Mornings began at around 5:30 a.m. It was hard to know exactly what time it was, because no one had a watch or a clock. Early in the morning, I would accompany my cousin to the mill to grind our corn into flour for tortillas. We would cook the tortillas over an open fireplace, which was built into the kitchen wall. That summer, I spent Sundays watching soccer games at the village soccer field. Each Sunday, a different neighboring team would challenge the local team. Sometimes the team would have to travel for the game and the whole village would travel with them. Talk about team spirit! During the week, my cousin and I would saddle our horses and ride up to the mountains and pick oranges. On Saturdays, my cousins and I would dress up and go to dances at the neighboring villages. There was always a wedding, a quinceañera [a coming of age ceremony] or a baptism. There was at least one dance every Saturday.

Once, my cousin and I went to four dances in one weekend! There were also horse races on the weekends. Sundays also meant that we would go into the city in the evening and hang out at the plaza to cenar, or have supper. We would buy fresh fruit smoothies and eat snacks. But the most fun was strolling around the plaza. The men walked counterclockwise and the women clockwise. The plaza would get packed with young people moving in circles. Occasionally, a man would hold out a flower to us as we passed to show his interest. If we were interested, we would take the flower. Then eventually, at some point there would be an invitation to leave the circle and move to one of the many surrounding benches to talk. That summer I celebrated my 21st birthday there. I was awakened that morning by a birthday serenata. The serenata group was a few guys from the village and they brought rocks and sticks. Endearing.

Mexico is on the verge of losing its culture.

I left at the end of the summer, not realizing that I would not return for 18 years. Even if I had realized that I wouldn't be returning for such a long time, I would never have guessed how drastically life in Mexico would have changed by the time I did eventually return.

Mexico Now

Finally, I returned in October 2005. I was so excited to visit, as if I was returning for a homecoming. However, everything had changed. The first sign that the village was not the same was waking up in the morning to the sound of trucks driving on the cobblestone streets. There had been very few cars when I had last been there. Now SUVs ruled the roads. There were practically no horses left. The sugarcane fields were gone. The corn fields were gone. I was there for 10 days and did not see anyone make tortillas. The sound of the mill was replaced by the trucks that came into the village from the big city of Guadalajara to sell tortillas and the dough for tortillas. The soccer field was overgrown with weeds. In fact, no one could remember when the last soccer game was played. The place where the horse races were held was no longer noticeable. The plaza was empty on Sundays, except for a few men standing around and an older couple sitting on one of the benches. It took me a while before I noticed there were no young adult men. There were teenagers and older men, but practically no men between 20 and 50. The sugarcane fields and the corn fields had been replaced with agave plants (from which tequila is distilled). I was told that agave required less manpower and was harvested every few years instead of every year. There were women of all ages and there were young children, but it seemed that fatherless families were more prevalent than not. I visited a few surrounding villages and found the same—no young adult men.

But, strangely enough, the houses were fancier, thanks to the materials shipped in from the United States. The village had a brand-new plaza and a brand-new church. There was a new kindergarten/daycare center, although the elementary school was the same. Almost all the homes had satellite television, a Dodge Ram truck, coffee makers, and even gas stoves. No more open fires. Even the traditional molcajete [stone grinder] had been replaced by the convenient blender. The village certainly prospered from having its labor force working for dollars in the United States. But the negative consequences of migration were evident in its daily life. The loss of the social customs of dating—a change culturally devastating in and of itself—was emblematic of the destruction of community and traditions and their replacement by the depersonalizing accumulation of commodities. A change to last forever.

It became obvious to me that the issue of immigration is not confined to the topic of cheap labor in the United States. Mexico and other Latin American countries are deeply affected by the loss of their young adult men. The absence of young adult men has created a damaging hole in the social infrastructure of Mexico. Mexico cannot possibly protect itself against a foreign invasion, whether military or cultural, when so many of its young able-bodied men are living and working in the United States. Nor can Mexico successfully push itself into a prominent position in world markets without their help. Worst of all, Mexico is on the verge of losing its culture—a way must be found to keep its men at home.

A Joint U.S.-Mexico Solution Is Needed

In its willing sacrifice of the most productive years in the lives of its men in the American labor market, Mexico has been heedlessly complicit in the uprooting of its cultural heritage, its characteristic ways of life, and its traditional values. On the other hand, the United States has accepted the sacrificial gift, has benefited greatly from it, but has remained largely unaware of the consequences, other than those which directly affect its economy. A workable and just U.S. immigration policy must take fully into account the consequences of emigration as well. Likewise, Mexico must no longer remain willfully ignorant of the consequences of unrestrained emigration and must negotiate agreements with the United States accordingly. Only if two countries work together, attentive to the indirect as well as the direct consequences of immigration, can the rancorous debate be transformed into a constructive discussion and an acceptable, lasting solution be found.

2

Emigration Has Positive and Negative Consequences in Mexico

Kevin Diaz

Kevin Diaz is the Washington correspondent at the Minneapolis Star Tribune. *He has won awards for his articles on globalization and immigration.*

Although Mexico's economy has greatly benefited from the estimated $20 billion that it receives each year in remittances from emigrants, the social and cultural downfalls have many questioning whether or not it is worth it. While this money has allowed the small Mexican town of Axochiapan to enjoy American luxuries such as cell phones and television sets, the town continues to lose its younger and more educated population to the United States. Mothers and wives have not seen their children or husbands for years, and grandparents have never met their grandchildren. Those that finally do return bring with them drug and alcohol addiction, creating more problems for the town. The citizens of Axochiapan hope that one day there will no longer be a need for emigration, but they do recognize the important role it currently plays in their standard of living.

A pickup truck with Minnesota plates bounced down the dirt road on the edge of town, raising clouds of reddish dust. It caught the eye of a grazing Brahman bull and disappeared behind a clutch of mango trees bordering a new subdivision, where tangles of steel reinforcing bars sprouted from the roofs of unfinished concrete block houses.

Many of the new houses were paid for with money sent by a secret workforce in Minnesota. By Mayor Leopoldo Rodriguez's estimate, almost a third of the town's workers have crossed the border—many of them illegally—and headed north to work in the Minneapolis–St. Paul metro area over the past 10 years.

The money they wire back arrives daily by police escort in armored trucks. Altogether, it comes to between $4 million and $7 million a month, according to money-transfer agencies in the Twin Cities region.

The cash has forged an economic link between Axochiapan and Minneapolis–St. Paul that is part of a global trend. It is changing Axochiapan, one household at a time.

The past decade has seen an explosion in emigration from poorer countries to the United States, the majority of it from Mexico.

Mexico Receives Billions in Remittances

Mexican immigrants, both legal and illegal, sent an estimated $20 billion back home last year [in 2005] from the United States. This rivals the $25 billion that Mexico takes in from oil exports.

The past decade has seen an explosion in emigration from poorer countries to the United States, the majority of it from Mexico.

It's not just happening in North America. More than $223 billion flows annually from migrant workers in the United States and other developed countries to poorer nations around the world. It's a flow that is transforming families, towns and, in some cases, entire countries, creating a new force in the global economy.

By dint of its migrant workforce in Minnesota, that global economy has come to Axochiapan.

Residents say the money pipeline has changed it from a provincial farm town to something almost reminiscent of the United States. There's a new hospital, built mostly with Minnesota money, and hundreds of new houses. American cars with Minnesota plates roar down the town's streets. And stores carry the latest CD players. All of which leaves residents worrying about prices inflated by the steady stream of American dollars.

This kind of money and labor flow has major consequences. In Axochiapan, the lure of American money has created a town where fathers and husbands are absent for years on end, women are left alone to raise the children, and the community is growing increasingly dependent on money made elsewhere.

Padre Miguel Franco Galicia, parish priest at the Church of San Pablo in Axochiapan, understands the lure of the green check.

Padre Miguel has visited Minneapolis several times to minister to his expatriate parishioners. He estimates that at least 60 percent of Axochiapan's population receives money from family members working in the United States, most of them in Minnesota.

"To be honest, I think there are more pluses than minuses, from an economic point of view," he said. "But the social devastation is enormous."

The Plus Side of Emigration

Axochiapan (pronounced Ah-sho-chee-AH-pahn), a town of about 30,000 in southern Mexico, has known little but poverty for centuries. People made a living by farming, or by working in the gypsum mines outside of town. The recent flow of Minnesota money has improved life. Pizza deliveries, aerobics studios and Internet cafes, alongside tortilla shops and taquerias, now serve an increasingly cosmopolitan population.

"Axochiapan would not be growing like it is without the people who go up north to work," said Antonio Estudillo, an aide to the mayor. "They suffer to bring a better life to their families." Estudillo knows this firsthand. He made enough money working for a money-transfer agency in Minneapolis four years ago [in 2002] to build a house for his family and open a stationery store for his wife.

Fathers and husbands are absent for years on end, [and] women are left alone to raise the children.

His friend Eduardo Navarro has seen business at his Axochiapan grocery store shoot up 50 percent in the past decade because of the money sent by migrants in America.

And then there's Jose Campos, who parlayed his wages from a dishwashing job in Minneapolis into a video arcade in Axochiapan.

Campos also runs a long-distance telephone service, charging cash for the use of his phone. Many of his customers call relatives in Minnesota.

Even though thousands of workers—primarily men—have left, Axochiapan's population has held steady. That's because the town's prosperity has become a magnet for farmers from the surrounding countryside, people who traditionally cultivated corn, sugar cane and onions.

They can be seen selling their produce beneath the colorful tarps of the town's open-air market, which has doubled in size over the past decade.

Now they represent a growing pool of potential new migrants.

The town has changed in other ways, too. Until recently, sewage and refuse piled up in dry creek beds along dusty side streets. There were no fire trucks and only one ambulance, which served a single overcrowded hospital near the bus station.

Now the town has money for sewer pipes and a new sewage treatment plant. Money is being raised for a second ambulance and a firetruck, courtesy of a group of Axochiapan expatriates in Minnesota.

Along with growth comes sprawl. Until a year ago, Axochiapan had no city planning department. Now the new planning director, Jaime Ramos, spends his days surveying the new building lots outside of town. He says that residential land is getting harder to afford, with a typical suburban lot now fetching $10,000—double the price of a decade ago.

The most conspicuous improvement is the gleaming white private hospital, the $3 million Clinica San Antonio, built almost entirely with Minnesota money. The hospital was built by the family that owns Envios America, a money-wire agency that handles a large part of the remittance market from the Twin Cities.

That money gives the town a future, said Envios America manager Fabiel Sanchez. "Five years ago, we didn't have the Internet and cell phones," he said. "People are better dressed now, and cement houses are replacing old adobe structures." Just about every week, young men set off from Axochiapan bound for Minnesota or other parts of the United States. Many go as soon as they graduate from high school.

Even though thousands of workers—primarily men— have left, Axochiapan's population has held steady.

The average weekly wage in Axochiapan is about 600 pesos, or $60.

That's about one-sixth of what most immigrants can make in the States.

"They see the things that people have who have worked in America," said Omar Lorenzo, a traveling salesman in Axochiapan. "They want to make money."

As Axochiapan prepared for a recent festival, Osvaldo Pliego pulled up to the Church of San Pablo. He was driving a Dodge minivan with Minnesota plates. In the back, he carried a load of drums, torches, and other things his band would need for that night's procession.

In Minnesota, where he worked construction for five years, the van had carried the tools of a different trade. Now, back in his hometown, he also uses the van as a taxi.

Like many of those driving newer American cars, Pliego couldn't have bought a car in Mexico. That's due in part to the difference in wages.

But another key reason is the financing, which is out of reach for most workers in this country town.

And the absence of a mortgage industry means that residents must pay cash for a house. A typical concrete-block home is about $15,000—far too expensive for the average farm worker, who makes about $10 a day.

Not All Mexicans Decide to Go North

Some people are starting to wonder how long the American money pipeline can last, particularly as political leaders in Washington push legislation to fortify America's border with Mexico.

Some economists also question whether this steady infusion of American dollars truly improves the fortunes of towns like Axochiapan, or makes them increasingly reliant on future generations of migrants. They fear that the flow of American money has fostered a culture of dependency that stifles local work.

Steven Camarota of the Center for Immigration Studies in Washington, D.C., says that the millions of dollars sent back to towns such as Axochiapan cause inflation and sap enterprise.

"It goes back to national aspiration," he said. "Sure, I can work in the fields, and sure, I can open up a business. But why don't I just go to Minneapolis illegally and work for a while?" Not everyone in Axochiapan feels the pull north. One who has resisted fiercely is Jose Sarafin, a 56-year-old gypsum miner with leathery hands and a sister and brother in Minneapolis.

"Yes, you can make money in America," he said. "But I'm proud of my work. We can live well here." Other locals decry the migration north as a continuation of Mexico's historic domination by the United States. They fear the weakening of traditions and the loss of their regional identity. "Unfortunately, those who leave are the young," said Isodoro Sanabria, a retired high school history teacher in Axochiapan. "Many get spoiled by life in America, or they start new families there, or only bring back problems like drug addiction." Sanabria worries about a drain on the town's talent and brains; those who head north, he said, seem to be the ones with the most ambition and education.

Studies by the Pew Hispanic Center indicate that those who go to the States have a higher level of education than the adult population of Mexico at large.

Sanabria also sees a creeping consumer culture in the Coke, Nikes and NFL jerseys he sees around town. Boys too young to spot Minnesota on a map can be found kicking soccer balls around while wearing purple [Minnesota Vikings then-quarterback] Daunte Culpepper jerseys, gifts from relatives abroad.

Mexican author Pablo Ruben Villalobos, who has written a poem praising Axochiapan's indigenous roots, says: "The money is a great help, but you have to think about who is left behind and what's lost."

The Downside of Emigration

Maria Luisa Morales is one of those left behind.

A widow and a church volunteer, she tends pigs and chickens in the backyard of her tidy stucco house next to a gypsum plant.

Her son Roberto sends money from Minneapolis, where he is a landscaper. She hasn't seen him in six years. "He said he would be gone a year," she said.

Roberto left Axochiapan when he was 20, following a girlfriend who had gone to Minneapolis. Since then, he has sent enough money back to help build a house for his sister.

But now he also has a house and a child in Minnesota—a grandson Morales has seen only in photos.

Her son is in the United States illegally, and visiting Mexico would mean another risky border crossing back to Minnesota. Morales is coming to terms with the thought that he might never come back. That thought fills her with dread.

"I ask him if he likes it there," she said. "It takes him a while to say yes, and in his silence I believe that the real answer is no."

The Rev. Lawrence Hubbard ("Padre Lorenzo") of Incarnation Catholic Church in Minneapolis and Padre Miguel of Axochiapan pray with many of the same families, separated by 2,000 miles and an international border.

Some of their immigrant parishioners call the priests the glue that holds the two cities together.

Both men say they try to discourage the migration and family separation, even though they understand the reasons behind it.

"Lots of people expect to come here (to Minnesota), work and then go back," Padre Lorenzo warned. "That's the ideal, and it does happen. But it's not that common."

Studies show that a third or more of the migrants go home again, but increasingly more are staying in the United States—or are trying to stay.

The sight of half-constructed houses in Axochiapan, the ones with the rusting reinforcing bars jutting out of unfinished concrete walls, are a testament to broken dreams—or permanent detours to America for workers who have not returned.

The danger of romantic betrayal and family abandonment is very real in a population of young men far from home.

"If you're a man (in America), it's hard to be faithful to your wife in Mexico," said Padre Lorenzo. "You have to live a life of abstinence." Depression is a common affliction for the migrants he counsels. The same is true for migrants' families in Axochiapan who seek out Padre Miguel.

"America can offer success or failure," Padre Miguel said. "People go to the United States to find work, but they also find alcoholism, drugs and family breakup. They make money, but they lose sight of God." Still, he knows that it's the desire for modern housing and a decent life that is driving the rush north.

"Their only sin," he said, "is they want to work to make a better life for their families."

The danger of romantic betrayal and family abandonment is very real in a population of young men far from home.

A New Yet Unaffordable Hospital

As the Minnesota money rolls in and the standard of living in Axochiapan improves, some hope that the emigration will eventually end. There is no doubt that for some, life already is better. The middle class in Axochiapan is growing, and residents are taking advantage of amenities such as the new private hospital.

Clinica San Antonio charges, on average, $7 to see a doctor and $50 per day for a private room. The government hospital, on the other hand, is free.

San Antonio has cool, spacious halls and modern equipment, most of which was purchased in Minnesota. While its rates are beyond the means of many of Axochiapan's residents, there are also plenty who can afford it; clinic directors say they see about 1,000 patients a month.

When Raul Pliego Sanchez and his wife, Luz Elena, were preparing for the birth of their first child, they chose San Antonio. He is an accountant in Axochiapan and earned the money to pay for his schooling by working as a busboy at the Mall of America [in suburban Minneapolis].

He hopes his new daughter—born in January [2006] by Caesarean section in San Antonio's cavernous new operating room—never has to go to America to earn a living.

"My wish," he said, "is for my children to stay in Mexico."

A Tribute to Those Who Have Left

Leopoldo Rodriguez, Axochiapan's mayor, made his money the old-fashioned way—he owns a gypsum plant outside of town. He's a traditionalist who wears a white cowboy hat, but he doesn't begrudge residents the American money that has eclipsed the town's historic reliance on mining and farming.

He has watched as people's lives have changed and grown modern.

"Before, it was rare to see somebody with a television in their house," he said. "Now, even the poorest people have television." To recognize the changes, he plans a memorial for those who have left and risked so much. He's asking townsfolk to donate discarded keys and other bits of scrap metal to cast a statue to El Migrante—the migrant.

It will depict a man carrying a suitcase, looking back over his shoulder at his wife and children. Behind them will be the figure of Mother Mexico.

"I thought of it as a symbol of their importance," Rodriguez said.

"These people are improving this city."

3

The Mexican Government Must Decrease Dependence on Remittances

Allan Wall

Allan Wall is an American and has been teaching English in Mexico since 1991. He has written articles about many aspects of Mexican life, such as Mexican politics, culture, and emigration.

With new Mexican president Felipe Calderón taking office, many worry that he will be as obsessed with emigration as the previous president, Vicente Fox. Although he has already been discussing emigration quite a bit, he insists that emigration will not be the focus of Mexico's relationship with the United States. However, with remittances playing such a large role in Mexico's economy, politicians need more of an incentive to fight to keep their fellow countrymen at home. The question is do remittances actually play a crucial role in Mexico's development? Michoacan, one of Mexico's least-developed states, proves exactly the opposite, despite the one in ten ratio of households that receive remittances. The new president would be better served to improve on such matters as the taxation system and developing a real federalism, giving Mexican states more freedom to manage their own revenues. This would be a step in the right direction in stopping the counterproductive remedy of emigration.

Will Felipe Calderón, scheduled to become Mexico's president on December 1st [2006], be as obsessed with emigration as President Vicente Fox has been for six years?

Allan Wall, "Will Calderon Also Be Obsessed with Mexican Emigration?" *Banderas News*, November 2006. Reproduced by permission.

Fox was obsessed with the emigration question and allowed it to gobble up valuable time and political capital, which would have been better spent to improve Mexico's economy rather than figuring out how to get more Mexicans out of Mexico.

Felipe Calderón has already been talking a lot about emigration, and in that respect he seems to be following the Fox game plan. On the other hand, Calderón has indicated that migration will not be the "central axis" of U.S.-Mexican relations.

The recent U.S. congressional elections open the possibility that President George W. Bush and a Democratic Congress will be able to give amnesty to illegal aliens and increase legal immigration. Yet the 2006 congressional election was not really a referendum on immigration, but a rejection of Republican incompetence.

As long as Mexican governments . . . can keep Mexicans crossing the border it will relieve pressure on the Mexican government.

It's significant that no winning congressional candidate campaigned on a pro-amnesty platform. The 2008 primary season is less than two years away, and things could change once again.

By investing so much capital on the immigration question, a Mexican president is staking his future on a question that can be reversed by the U.S. electorate.

However, from the Mexican perspective a more basic question remains. Regardless of what U.S. politicians might do about immigration policy, is the continuance of mass emigration in the long-term economic and social interests of Mexico?

Emigration Is a Safety Valve

Certainly emigration generates a lot of money for Mexico in remittances. In fact, remittance money may soon surpass oil revenue as Mexico's largest legal source of income.

Emigration also provides Mexico's leaders with a safety valve. As long as Mexican governments (of whatever party) can keep Mexicans crossing the border it will relieve pressure on the Mexican government.

And that, alas, is part of the problem. What incentives do Mexico's leaders have to reform the Mexican economy as long as the emigration safety valve looms so large?

What about those remittances? Mexico is now the world's biggest source of emigration (the largest exporter of human beings), and the 3rd largest recipient (after China and India) of remittance money.

Remittances do provide a social safety net. But as motors of economic development, remittances are not too effective, say several experts.

Remittances Not Key to Economy

For example, Alfonso Sandoval, spokesman for the United Nations Population Fund (UNFPA), says that remittances are not incentives for productive development in the Mexican regions that receive them. And none other than Mexican central bank chief Guillermo Ortiz said something quite similar, that remittances provide a social safety net but are not a key lubricant of the Mexican economy.

For a concrete example, consider Felipe Calderón's home state of Michoacan.

Of all Mexican states, Michoacan has the highest dependency on remittances, with one out of ten households receiving them. Now if the remittances-are-great theory were correct, wouldn't Michoacan be booming? On the contrary, it is one of Mexico's least developed states and continues to expel large amounts of emigrants. The same is true of other states with high remittance-dependency, such as Zacatecas, Guanajuato and Durango.

Rather than solving Mexico's problems, remittances just perpetuate the viciousness of underdevelopment and encourage more Mexicans to emigrate. If Calderón wants real economic development he needs to move Mexico away from its heroin-like addiction to remittances.

And there are plenty of areas to improve.

Better Ways to Fix Mexico's Economy

As a former energy secretary, Calderón knows what a mess PEMEX (Mexico's oil monopoly) is in. Politically, any sort of privatization or even semi-privatization would unleash a firestorm of protest, but something has to be done.

Rather than solving Mexico's problems, remittances just perpetuate the viciousness of underdevelopment and encourage more Mexicans to emigrate.

Mexico's enormous informal economy is in reality an economic resource, and ways should be found to legalize it and bring it into the formal economy.

Taxation must be made more efficient, as estimates put Mexican tax evasion at 40 percent.

Calderón could work to achieve a real federalism, in which Mexican states have more leeway in managing their own revenues, rather than a one-size-fits-all approach to the economy.

These are just a few of the areas that Calderón and the new Mexican Congress can concentrate on to improve Mexico's economy. It would be much better than the tired and counter-productive remedy of sending more and more Mexicans northward.

4

Mexico Is Trying New Methods to Influence U.S. Immigration Policy

Manuel Roig-Franzia

Manuel Roig-Franzia has been a staff writer for the Washington Post *since 2000 and travels throughout the Caribbean and Latin America for the newspaper. He is based in Mexico City.*

Although Mexican president Felipe Calderón wants immigration reform in the United States, just as past Mexican presidents have wanted, he is taking a subtler approach in an attempt to slow the rate of emigration from Mexico. Instead he is focusing on improving Mexico's economy by actively crushing drug cartels in hopes that it will boost tourism. He is also encouraging foreign investment, asking international companies to bid on contracts to build toll roads, which in turn would create thousands of jobs. However, while Calderón is attempting to improve the standard of living in Mexico, it is still going to take a while to turn the emphasis away from emigration, especially when he is still pushing so adamantly for immigration reform, attacking proposals to build more fences along the border.

When President [George W.] Bush lands in the Yucatan colonial city of Merida on Monday night [March 19, 2007], he will encounter a new Mexican government that wants the same thing the old one wanted: comprehensive immigration reform in the United States.

Shifting Focus Away from Immigration

What's different is that Mexican President Felipe Calderón, in office since December [2006], is trying a slower and subtler approach. Calderón and his lieutenants have even invented a buzzword to define their strategy, saying they will "desmigratizar" the bilateral agenda, or remove immigration from the forefront of U.S.-Mexico relations.

"He's having to find a new vocabulary," said Juan Hernández, who headed a cabinet-level office for Mexicans living abroad during the administration of Calderón's predecessor, Vicente Fox.

Calderón has spoken out against U.S. border policy, calling border fences "deplorable" and predicting that security measures will lead to an increase in migrant deaths. Still, the president's top aides say he is convinced that, to achieve immigration reform, he must demonstrate to the U.S. Congress that Mexico is willing to address the factors propelling illegal migration, especially the country's weak job market and low standard of living.

The president is also pressing for human rights reforms on his nation's troubled border with Guatemala, in an attempt to avert accusations that Mexico has mistreated migrants.

Calderón's biggest initiative has been a far-flung effort to crush drug cartels, whose barbaric turf wars have discouraged tourism and foreign investment.

Given the dimensions of Calderón's challenge—the minimum wage is $4.60 a day and the World Bank estimates that more than 40 percent of Mexicans live in poverty—his allies say they do not expect to produce enough tangible results to spur immigration reform in the United States during the final two years of the Bush administration.

"Maybe we won't succeed in the near term, but we could succeed in the medium term," Alejandro Landero Gutiérrez, a member of Calderón's National Action Party who serves on the foreign relations committee of the Mexican Congress, said in an interview. "We're building this brick by brick. Our expectations are much more reserved."

Calderón visited Bush at the White House in November, during a pre-inauguration international tour. "I didn't come to the United States looking for Americans or this country's government to solve problems we have in Mexico, which we will have to solve on our own," he said after the meeting.

Attempting to Create More Jobs

Since he took office, Calderón's biggest initiative has been a far-flung effort to crush drug cartels, whose barbaric turf wars have discouraged tourism and foreign investment. He has sent Mexican troops and federal police to resorts, such as Acapulco, and to hot spots along the border, such as Tijuana and Monterrey.

While the military offensive has produced mixed results— there have been some arrests, but violence persists—Calderón has also been encouraging foreign investment. He recently proposed inviting international companies to bid on contracts to build private toll roads, which could create thousands of jobs.

He is also pursuing a domestic agenda aimed at curbing emigration by improving social services and generating jobs. In January, Calderón launched a program that will give cash incentives to companies that hire first-time job holders. His administration also projects spending 6.7 percent more on education this year than Fox's did last year, 26.8 percent more on public health and 27.6 percent more on social development programs, according to statistics provided by Landero Gutiérrez.

"In marginalized communities, after paying for the basic costs of education, health care and food, people are left with nothing, and they're forced to migrate," Landero Gutiérrez said.

But shifting the focus away from immigration is not a simple endeavor. U.S. immigration policies have made Bush profoundly unpopular in Mexico and other Latin American countries. A Zogby International poll published in January by *Newsweek* magazine indicated that two-thirds of prominent Mexicans—including politicians and business people—view relations with the United States as "poor." In the meantime, there are strong pressures in Mexico to find ways to improve living conditions—and perhaps attain legal status—for the estimated 6 million Mexicans living illegally in the United States.

Dan Lund, a Mexico City pollster, said Calderón, whose party falls well short of a majority in Congress, is hampered by "a divided house" on the question of how much emphasis to place on immigration. Jorge Castañeda, who was foreign minister under Fox and famously said Mexico wanted "the whole enchilada" of immigration reforms, has disagreed, calling Calderón's strategy "foolishness."

Two-thirds of prominent Mexicans—including politicians and business people—view relations with the United States as "poor."

Mexico Will Continue to Push for Reforms

While de-emphasizing immigration reform, Calderón has also given signals that he won't stop trying to cajole American lawmakers. Before leaving for the United States, Calderón's new ambassador to Washington, Arturo Sarukhan, told reporters that Mexico would use its U.S. diplomatic corps to lobby for reforms.

"We are going to put into place the same kind of diplomatic and lobbying effort that we did in the early 1990s when NAFTA was being decided," Sarukhan said last month [February 2007], referring to the North American Free Trade Agreement.

Calderón has sometimes departed from his strategy of shifting immigration out of the spotlight in U.S.-Mexico relations. In July, during his first news briefing, he attacked proposals to build more fences along the border.

As months passed, his rhetoric became even stronger. During a visit to Canada in October, Calderón said, "Humanity committed a grave error by constructing the Berlin Wall, and I am sure that today the United States is committing a grave error in constructing a wall along our northern border."

5

European Emigration Is Linked to Its Welfare Systems

Paul Belien

Paul Belien is the editor of the Brussels Journal, a Belgian blog, as well as an adjunct fellow of the Hudson Institute in New York.

In the year 2006, more than 155,000 Germans left their native country, which is a much higher number than the number of those coming into Germany. While the people leaving are well educated and highly motivated, the ones coming in are mostly poor and uneducated. This situation is the same in many other European countries, such as the Netherlands where the Dutch saw a spike in emigration after the assassinations of two political figureheads, lending credence to the idea that much of this emigration is because many have lost faith in their government. Another issue plaguing Europe is the welfare system, which takes money from their skilled and educated workers to pay for the uneducated, unemployed newcomers from third world countries, which offers another reason for the rise in emigration: The only way to save Europe is to make a drastic reform to the welfare system.

L ast year [2006] more than 155,000 Germans emigrated from their native country. Since 2004 the number of ethnic Germans who leave each year is greater than the number of immigrants moving in. While the emigrants are highly motivated and well educated, "those coming in are mostly poor, untrained and hardly educated," says Stephanie Wahl of the German Institute for Economics.

In a survey conducted in 2005 among German university students, 52 percent said they would rather leave their native country than remain there. By "voting with their feet," young, educated Germans affirm that Germany has no future to offer them and their children. As one couple who moved to the United States told the newspaper *Die Welt*: "Here our children have a future in which they will not have to fear unemployment and social decline." There are two main reasons why so-called "ethno-Germans" emigrate. Some complain that the tax rates in Germany are so high that it is no longer worthwhile working for a living there. Others indicate they no longer feel at home in a country whose cultural appearance is changing dramatically.

The situation is similar in other countries in Western Europe. Since 2003, emigration has exceeded immigration to the Netherlands. In 2006, the Dutch saw more than 130,000 compatriots leave. The rise in Dutch emigration peaked after the assassinations of [politician] Pim Fortuyn and [film director] Theo van Gogh. This indicates that the flight from Europe is related to a loss of confidence in the future of nations which have taken in the Trojan horse of Islamism, but which, unlike the Trojans, lack the guts to fight.

Elsewhere in Western Europe immigration currently still surpasses emigration, though emigration figures are rising fast. In Belgium the number of emigrants surged by 15 percent in the past years. In Sweden, 50,000 people packed their bags last year—a rise of 18 percent compared to the previous year and the highest number of Swedes leaving since 1892. In the United Kingdom, almost 200,000 British citizens move out every year.

Americans who think that the European welfare state is the model to follow would do well to ponder the question why, if Europe is so wonderful, Europeans are fleeing from it. European welfare systems are redistribution mechanisms, taking money from skilled and educated Europeans in order to give it to nonskilled newcomers from the Third World.

Young, educated Germans affirm that Germany has no future to offer them and their children.

Gunnar Heinsohn, a German sociologist at the University of Bremen, warns European governments that they are mistaken if they assume that qualified young ethnic Europeans will stay in Europe. "The really qualified are leaving," Mr. Heinsohn says. "The only truly loyal towards France and Germany are those who are living off the welfare system, because there is no other place in the world that offers to pay for them. . . . It is no wonder that young, hardworking people in France and Germany choose to emigrate," he explains. "It is not just that they have to support their own aging population. If we take 100 20-year-olds [in France or Germany], then the 70 [indigenous] Frenchmen and Germans also have to support 30 immigrants of their own age and their offspring. This creates dejection in the local population, particularly in France, Germany and the Netherlands. So they run away."

[In June 2007] François Fillon, the new French prime minister, said that "Europe is not Eldorado," emphasizing that his government intends to curb immigration by those who only seek welfare benefits. "Europe is hospitable, France is an immigration country and will continue to be so, but it will only accept foreigners prepared to integrate," he stressed. Europe cannot afford to be "Eldorado" for foreigners any longer, because it has stopped being "home" for thousands of its own educated children, now eagerly looking for opportunities to move to America, Canada, Australia or New Zealand—white European nations outside Europe.

European welfare systems are redistribution mechanisms, taking money from skilled and educated Europeans in order to give it to nonskilled newcomers.

While the fertility rate in France is 1.9 children per woman, two out of every five newborns in France are children of Arab or African immigrants. In Germany (fertility rate 1.37) 35 percent of all newborns have a non-German background. Paradoxically, fertility rates in Turkey, Morocco, Algeria, Tunisia, etc., are lower than among immigrants from these countries in Europe. "A woman in Tunisia has on average 1.7 children. In France she has six because the French government pays her to have them," Mr. Heinsohn explains. "Of course, the money was never intended to benefit Tunisian women in particular, but French women will not touch this money, whereas the Tunisian women are only too happy to. . . . For Danish and German women the welfare benefits are too low to be attractive. Not so for the immigrants. So, what we see in England, France, Germany and the Netherlands are immigrant women who take low-paid jobs which they supplement with public benefits. It is not a fantastic income but sufficient for them," he said.

Europe's welfare system is causing a perverse process of population replacement. If the Europeans want to save their culture, they will have to slay the welfare state.

6

Christian Emigration from Lebanon Gives Islam More Political Power There

Rana Fil

Rana Fil is a correspondent for the Boston Globe *and a contributor to other magazines such as* Newsweek.

Lebanese Christians are frustrated and feel that their political influence is being threatened. As they feel increasingly marginalized, the Muslim Sunni and Shiite sects are each united, which weakens Christian hegemony even more. In light of the disquiet among the government many Christians are leaving the country, lowering the percentage of Lebanese Christians to as little as 30 percent by some estimates. It is this lowering of the Christian population that will have the most profound effect on the political calculus, as it will only allow the Muslims to gain influence.

Lebanon's political stalemate was supposed to be resolved weeks ago. Instead it drags on, with [the December 2007] parliamentary session to elect a new head of state now postponed for the eighth time since September. And as the impasse continues, Lebanese Christians are becoming increasingly frustrated with what they see as an unprecedented threat to their political influence. "It is the first time in the history of Lebanon that Christians feel so demoralized," said Elie Haddad, Greek Catholic Archbishop of Saida and Deir el-Kamar. "I have never seen such despondency, even during the civil war."

The trigger for Lebanon's latest crisis is the ongoing dispute over finding a successor to pro-Syrian President Emile Lahoud, whose term expired Nov. 23. Parliamentary leaders have tentatively agreed on compromise candidate Gen. Michel Suleiman—but are still squabbling over how to amend the constitution for the army chief to assume his new position. For the country's Christians, however, the dispute over Suleiman has an even deeper significance. Many see it as underscoring the subsidiary role played by Christian leaders in Parliament's two main factions: the ruling, pro-Western March 14 coalition led by Sunni Muslim Saad Hariri and the Hizbullah-dominated opposition led by Shiite leader Hassan Nasrallah. "Christian leaders are divided among themselves at a time when the Shiites are united and the Sunnis are united," says Rajeh Khoury, a columnist at the daily *An-Nahar* newspaper. "The more divided they are the weaker their role is in Lebanese politics."

For many Christians these developments are fueling a new rush to leave the country. Church leaders say they are growing increasingly alarmed at the accelerating pace of emigration and what Greek Orthodox Archbishop of Mount Lebanon, Georges Khodr, calls "a visceral sense of their disappearance through emigration." Haddad says that large numbers of Christians are selling out if they can afford to leave and that others are staying "with total resignation to the current situation." Other clerics echo similar sentiments. "We see people rushing for visas, and emigration continues unabated," said Msgr. Boulos Nasrallah, of the Maronite [an Eastern Rite Roman Catholic Church] bishopric of Jbeil. "But we have faith that this is our country."

Nobody knows exactly how many Christians have left because of the political sensitivity over the collection of statistics. Christians now make up less than 40 percent of Lebanon's population—indeed, some estimates put it as low as 30 percent—and they fear that confirmation of their declining numbers will lead to Muslim demands for increased political representation. Christians aren't the only ones who are leaving, but it's their departure that could have the most profound effect on Lebanon's sensitive political calculus. Riad Tabbarah, a political analyst and head of the Center for Development Studies and Projects, says that Lebanon's economic woes mean that emigration is affecting all religious communities "almost equally," but because Christians are a minority in the Arab world they are "particularly concerned about their emigration."

Church leaders say they are growing increasingly alarmed at the accelerating pace of emigration.

Can Suleiman soothe the situation enough to stem this trend? A Maronite Christian, he remains a cipher to many Lebanese. As head of the army, he has trodden a careful middle ground between the country's anti-Syrian rulers and its Syrian-backed opposition. His actions seem to have been evenhanded, aimed at keeping the army neutral and united during turbulent times. He did not try to put down the mass street demonstrations that forced Syria to withdraw from Lebanon in 2005, but he did issue a statement absolving Syria of any connection to the Fatah al-Islam radicals who clashed with his troops in the Nahr el-Bared Palestinian refugee camp in Tripoli [in 2007]. Perhaps more significantly, Suleiman has succeeded in maintaining good relations with Hizbullah even as he deployed his army to the militant group's strongholds in south Lebanon in accordance with the U.N. resolution that ended the 2006 Israel-Hizbullah war.

Still, Suleiman's nomination has done little to assuage Christian leaders in the ruling March 14 group. Some suggest that he is the man Syria wants in the job; others complain that they were not consulted prior to his being suggested publicly as a candidate. Exacerbating the fears of the Christian parliamentarians are suggestions that Hizbullah may try to amend the Taif Accord that ended Lebanon's 1975–1990 civil war. That agreement gave Muslims and Christians equal representation in Parliament and government. Under the power-sharing system, the president has to be a Maronite, the prime minister a Sunni and the speaker of parliament a Shiite Muslim. According to the March 14 Christians, Iran—which also backs Hizbullah—is trying to review the 50-50 split, suggesting instead that Lebanon change its constitution to reduce Christian representation from half to a third. The remaining two-thirds would be assigned to Muslims, with an equal split between Sunni and Shiite. Hizbullah denies these claims, insisting it remains committed to the agreement. "We did not ask for anything outside the Taif Accord," says Hizbullah parliamentarian Mohammad Fneish. "To say that we want such an amendment is an attempt to stoke fears."

For many Christians, remaining in Lebanon is a matter of faith.

Rhetoric aside, there is little doubt that fears *are* being stoked—largely because Hizbullah is maintaining its refusal to disarm. That, in turn, is continuing to fuel Christian flight. "All my friends have left the country," says Abeer Antonios, a 28-year-old saleswoman at a clothing store in Beirut. "Lebanon will soon be an Islamic state." Antonios says she too plans to leave if she can get a job offer from the outside. Others share her frustration. "Christians are being trampled because our leaders cannot agree with each other," says Annie Astounian, 50. "No one is working for the interest of the country." Still, for many Christians, remaining in Lebanon is a matter of faith. Joseph Chaccour, 36, says that his religious beliefs prevent him from emigrating. "No one will remove the Christians from Lebanon," he says. "Jesus and the Virgin Mary want us to stay."

7

No Country Benefits from Brain Drain

Sam Vaknin

Sam Vaknin, Ph.D., is the author of Malignant Self Love: Narcissism Revisited *and* After the Rain: How the West Lost the East. *He has been a columnist for several publications, including the* Global Politician, *as well as the editor of mental health and Central and East Europe categories in* The Open Directory *and* Suite 101.

Half of 150 million immigrants dispersed throughout the world are illegal aliens who have fled war, terrorism, poverty, and unemployment. While the primary destination is America or the European Union (EU), many end up in places like Africa and Asia. The United Nations Population Division reports that the EU would need to bring in 1.6 million immigrants a year to maintain its current level of working age population and nine times as many to maintain a stable workers to retirees ratio. In light of these and other statistics, Europe has become stricter on its immigration policies. They have realized that many of those leaving its countries are the educated and skilled population, while the few that are entering are poor and uneducated. The European Commission is ready to take steps in an attempt to lure some of those that have left back by upgrading their universities and research facilities. An agreement needs to be made that changes brain drain to brain exchange so that every country benefits from their investment.

Sam Vaknin, Ph.D., "Migration and Brain Drain," *Global Politician*, October 9, 2006. Reproduced by permission.

Human trafficking and people smuggling are multi-billion dollar industries. At least 50% of the 150 million immigrants the world over are illegal aliens. There are 80 million migrant workers found in virtually every country. They flee war, urban terrorism, crippling poverty, corruption, authoritarianism, nepotism, cronyism, and unemployment. Their main destinations are the EU [European Union] and the USA—but many end up in lesser countries in Asia or Africa.

The International Labour Organization (ILO) published the following figures in 1997:

Africa had 20 million migrant workers, North America—17 million, Central and South America—12 million, Asia—7 million, the Middle East—9 million, and Europe—30 million.

Immigrants make up 15% of staid Switzerland's population, 9% of Germany's and Austria's, 7.5% of France's (though less than 4% of multi-cultural Blairite [i.e., under prime minister Tony Blair] Britain). There are more than 15 million people born in Latin America living in the States. According to the American Census Bureau, foreign workers comprise 13% of the workforce (up from 9% in 1990). A million have left Russia for Israel. In this past century, the world has experienced its most sweeping wave of both voluntary and forced immigration—and it does not seem to have abated.

According to the United Nations Population Division, the EU would need to import 1.6 million migrant workers annually to maintain its current level of working age population. But it would need almost 9 times as many to preserve a stable workers to pensioners ratio.

Migrant workers are often discriminated against and abused and many are expelled intermittently.

The EU may cope with this shortage by simply increasing labour force participation (74% in labour-short Netherlands, for instance). Or it may coerce its unemployed (and women) into low-paid and 3-d (dirty, dangerous, and difficult) jobs. Or it may prolong working life by postponing retirement.

These are not politically palatable decisions. Yet, a wave of xenophobia [a dislike or fear of anything foreign] that hurtled lately across a startled Europe—from Austria to Denmark—won't allow the EU to adopt the only other solution: mass (though controlled and skill-selective) migration.

What the Statistics Mean

As a result, Europe has recently tightened its admission (and asylum) policies even more than it had in the 1970's. It bolted and shut its gates to primary (economic) migration. Only family reunifications are permitted. Well over 80% of all immigrants to Britain are women joining their husbands, or children joining their father. Migrant workers are often discriminated against and abused and many are expelled intermittently.

Still, economic migrants—lured by European riches—keep pouring in illegally (about half a million every year—to believe The Centre for Migration Policy Development in Vienna). Europe is the target of twice as many illegal migrants as the USA. Many of them (known as "labour tourists") shuttle across borders seasonally, or commute between home and work sometimes daily. Hence the EU's apprehension at allowing free movement of labour from the candidate countries and the "transition periods" (really moratoria) it wishes to impose on them following their long postponed accession.

According to the American Census Bureau's March 2002 "Current Population Survey", 20% of all US residents are of "foreign stock" (one quarter of them Mexican). They earn less than native-born Americans and are less likely to have health insurance. They are (on average) less educated (only 67% of immigrants age 25 and older completed high school compared to 87% of native-born Americans). Their median income, at $36,000 is 10% lower and only 49% of them own a home (compared to 67% of households headed by native-born Americans). The averages mask huge disparities between Asians and Hispanics, though. Still, these ostensibly dismal figures constitute a vast improvement over comparable data in the country of origin.

But these are the distant echoes of past patterns of migration. Traditional immigration is becoming gradually less attractive. Immigrants who came to Canada between 1985–1998 earn only 66% of the wages of their predecessors. Labour force participation of immigrants fell to 68% (1996) from 86% (1981).

A Change in the Type of Emigrant

While most immigrants until the 1980's were poor, uneducated, and unskilled—the current lot is middle-class, reasonably affluent, well educated, and highly skilled. This phenomenon—the exodus of elites from all the developing and less developed countries—is called "brain drain", or "brain hemorrhage" by its detractors (and "brain exchange" or "brain mobility" by its proponents). These metaphors conjure up images of the inevitable outcomes of some mysterious processes, the market's invisible hand plucking the choicest and teleporting them to more abundant grounds.

Yet, this is far from being true. The developed countries, once a source of such emigration themselves (more than 100,000 European scientists left for the USA in the wake of the Second World War)—actively seek to become its destination by selectively attracting only the skilled and educated citizens of developing countries. They offer them higher salaries, a legal status (however contingent), and tempting attendant perks. The countries of origin cannot compete, able to offer only $50 a month salaries, crumbling universities, shortages of books and lab equipment, and an intellectual wasteland.

The European Commission had this to say [in September 2006]:

"The Commission proposes, therefore, that the Union recognize the realities of the situation of today: that on the one hand migratory pressures will continue and that on the other hand in a context of economic growth and a declining and aging population, Europe needs immigrants. In this context our objective is not the quantitative increase in migratory flows but better management in qualitative terms so as to realize more fully the potential of immigrants' admitted."

And the EU's Social and Employment Commission added, as it forecast a deficit of 1.7 million workers in Information and Communications Technologies throughout the Union:

"A declining EU workforce due to demographic changes suggests that immigration of third country nationals would also help satisfy some of the skill needs [in the EU]. Reforms of tax benefit systems may be necessary to help people make up their minds to move to a location where they can get a job . . . while ensuring that the social objectives of welfare systems are not undermined."

While most immigrants until the 1980's were poor, uneducated, and unskilled—the current lot is middle-class, reasonably affluent, well educated, and highly skilled.

In Hong Kong, the "Admission of Talents Scheme" (1999) and "The Admission of Mainland Professionals Scheme" (May 2001) allow mainlanders to enter it for 12 month periods, if they: "Possess outstanding qualifications, expertise or skills which are needed but not readily available in Hong Kong. They must have good academic qualifications, normally a doctorate degree in the relevant field."

The Impact on the Receiving Countries

According the January 2002 issue of "Migration News", even now, with unemployment running at almost 6%, the US H1-B visa program allows 195,000 foreigners with academic degrees to enter the US for up to 6 years and "upgrade" to immigrant status while in residence. Many H1-B visas were cancelled due to the latest economic slowdown—but the US provides other kinds of visas (E type) to people who invest in its territory by, for instance, opening a consultancy.

The UK has just implemented the Highly Skilled Migrant Programme which allows "highly mobile people with the special talents that are required in a modern economy" to enter the UK for a period of one year (with indefinite renewal). Even xenophobic Japan allowed in 222,000 qualified foreigners [in 2005] (double the figure in 1994).

Germany has absorbed 10,000 computer programmers (mainly from India and Eastern Europe) since July 2000. Ireland was planning to import twenty times as many over 7 years. . . . According to *The Economist*, more than 10,000 teachers have left Ecuador since 1998. More than half of all Ghanaian medical doctors have emigrated (120 in 1998 alone). More than 60% of all Ethiopian students abroad never return. There are 64,000 university educated Nigerians in the USA alone. More than 43% of all Africans living in North America have acquired at least a bachelor's degree.

[Researchers] Barry Chiswick and Timothy Hatton demonstrated that, as the economies of poor countries improve, emigration increases because people become sufficiently wealthy to finance the trip.

The Effect on the Sending Countries

Poorer countries invest an average of $50,000 of their painfully scarce resources in every university graduate—only to witness most of them emigrate to richer places. The haves-not thus end up subsidizing the haves by exporting their human capital, the prospective members of their dwindling elites, and the taxes they would have paid had they stayed put. The formation of a middle class is often irreversibly hindered by an all-pervasive brain drain.

Politicians in some countries decry this trend and deride those emigrating. In a famous interview on state TV, the late prime minister of Israel, Yitzhak Rabin, described them as "a fallout of the jaded". But in many impoverished countries, local kleptocracies [governments that seek personal gain at the expense of the governed] welcome the brain drain as it also drains the country of potential political adversaries.

Emigration also tends to decrease competitiveness. It increases salaries at home by reducing supply in the labour market (and reduces salaries at the receiving end, especially for unskilled workers). Illegal migration has an even stronger downward effect on wages in the recipient country—illegal aliens tend to earn less than their legal compatriots. The countries of origin, whose intellectual elites are depleted by the brain drain, are often forced to resort to hiring (expensive) foreigners. African countries spend more than $4 billion annually on foreign experts, managers, scientists, programmers, and teachers.

The formation of a middle class is often irreversibly hindered by an all-pervasive brain drain.

Still, remittances by immigrants to their relatives back home constitute up to 10% of the GDP [gross domestic product] of certain countries—and up to 40% of national foreign exchange revenues. The World Bank estimates that Latin American and Caribbean nationals received $15 billion in remittances in 2000—ten times the 1980 figure. This may well be a gross underestimate. Mexicans alone remitted $6.7 billion in the first 9 months of 2001 (though job losses and reduced hours may have since adversely affected remittances). The IADB [Inter-American Development Bank] thinks that remittances will total $300 billion in the next decade (Latin American immigrants send home c. 15% of their wages).

Official remittances (many go through unmonitored money transfer channels, such as the Asian Hawala network) are larger than all foreign aid combined. *The Economist* calculates that workers' remittances in Latin America and the Caribbean are three times as large as aggregate foreign aid and larger than export proceeds. Yet, this pecuniary [money-related] flood is mostly used to finance the consumption of basics: staple foods, shelter, maintenance, clothing. It is nonproductive capital.

Only a tiny part of the money ends up as investment. Countries—from Mexico to Israel, and from Macedonia to Guatemala—are trying to tap into the considerable wealth of their diasporas [dispersed populations] by issuing remittance-bonds, by offering tax holidays, one-stop-shop facilities, business incubators, and direct access to decision makers—as well as matching investment funds.

Attempts to Correct Brain Drain

Migrant associations are sprouting all over the Western world, often at the behest of municipal authorities back home. The UNDP [United Nations Development Programme], the International Organization of Migration (IOM), as well as many governments (e.g., Israel, China, Venezuela, Uruguay, Ethiopia), encourage expatriates to share their skills with their counterparts in their country of origin. The thriving hi-tech industries in Israel, India, Ireland, Taiwan, and South Korea were founded by returning migrants who brought with them not only capital to invest and contacts—but also entrepreneurial skills and cutting edge technologies.

Thailand established in 1997, within the National Science and Technology Development Agency, a 2.2 billion baht [Thai currency] project called "Reverse the Brain Drain". Its aim is to "use the 'brain' and 'connections' of Thai professionals living overseas to help in the development of Thailand, particularly in science and technology."

The OECD [Organization for Economic Co-operation and Development] ("International Mobility of the Highly Skilled") believes that:

"More and more highly skilled workers are moving abroad for jobs, encouraging innovation to circulate and helping to boost economic growth around the globe."

But it admits that a "greater co-operation between sending and receiving countries is needed to ensure a fair distribution of benefits".

The key to a pacific and prosperous future lies in a multilateral agreement between brain-exporting, brain-importing, and transit countries.

The OECD noted, in its "Annual Trends in International Migration, 2001" that (to quote its press release):

Migration involving qualified and highly qualified workers rose sharply between 1999 and 2000, helped by better employment prospects and the easing of entry conditions. Instead of granting initial temporary work permits only for one year, as in the past, some OECD countries, particularly in Europe, have been issuing them for up to five years and generally making them renewable. Countries such as Australia and Canada, where migration policies were mainly aimed at permanent settlers, are also now favoring temporary work permits valid for between three and six years. . . . In addition to a general increase in economic prosperity, one of the main factors behind the recent increase in worker migration has been the development of information technology, a sector where in 2000 there was a shortage of around 850,000 technicians in the US and nearly 2 million in Europe . . .

But the OECD underplays the importance of brain drain:

"Fears of a 'brain drain' from developing to technologically advanced countries may be exaggerated, given that many professionals do eventually return to their country of origin. To avoid the loss of highly qualified workers, however, developing countries need to build their own innovation and research facilities. . . . China, for example, has recently launched a program aimed at developing 100 selected universities into world-class research centers. Another way to ensure return . . . could be to encourage students to study abroad while making study grants conditional on the student's return home."

The key to a pacific and prosperous future lies in a multilateral agreement between brain-exporting, brain-importing, and transit countries. Such an agreement should facilitate the sharing of the benefits accruing from migration and "brain exchange" among host countries, countries of origin, and transit countries. In the absence of such a legal instrument, resentment among poorer nations is likely to grow even as the mushrooming needs of richer nations lead them to snatch more and more brains from their already woefully depleted sources.

8

There Are Benefits to Brain Drain

Michael A. Clemens and David McKenzie

Michael A. Clemens is an affiliated associate professor of public policy at Georgetown University and a research fellow at the Center for Global Development. David McKenzie is a research affiliate for Innovations for Poverty Action, a fellow of the Center for Research and Analysis of Migration, and a senior economist of the World Bank's Development Research Group.

Several of the same countries that receive aid from and participate in trade with the United States are also complaining about "brain drain" or the loss of their educated people to the richer countries; however, one must take into consideration some facts in regard to that assumption, such as the fact that while the Philippines is the largest exporter of nurses, they still have a higher ratio of nurses working in their country than Britain does. As far as wasting money on those who emigrate, there are facts that must be considered here as well, such as the fact that many receive their education outside of their native country and pay for their education themselves. Many also work in their own countries long enough to provide a substantial return on the investment. The term "brain drain" implies that the emigration of skilled workers is a bad thing, but new research proves otherwise.

Many of the same countries courted by the United States through aid and trade deals complain bitterly of the "brain drain" of their doctors, scientists, and engineers to the

United States and other rich countries. If correct, these complaints would mean that current immigration policy amounts to counterproductive foreign policy. Thankfully, however, the flow of skilled emigrants from poor to rich parties can actually benefit both parties.

This common idea that skilled emigration amounts to "stealing" requires a cartoonish set of assumptions about developing countries. First, it requires us to assume that developing countries possess a finite stock of skilled workers, a stock depleted by one for every departure. In fact, people respond to the incentives created by migration: Enormous numbers of skilled workers from developing countries have been induced to acquire their skills by the opportunity of high earnings abroad. This is why the Philippines, which sends more nurses abroad than any other developing country, still has more nurses per capita *at home* than Britain does. Recent research has also shown that a sudden, large increase in skilled emigration from a developing country to a skill-selective destination can cause a corresponding sudden increase in skill acquisition in the source country.

Second, believing that skilled emigration amounts to theft from the poor requires us to assume that skilled workers themselves are not poor. In Zambia, a nurse has to get by on less than $1,500 per year—measured at U.S. prices, not Zambian ones—and a doctor must make ends meet with less than $5,500 per year, again at U.S. prices. If these were your annual wages, facing U.S. price levels, you would likely consider yourself destitute. Third, believing that a person's choice to emigrate constitutes "stealing" requires problematic assumptions about that person's rights. The United Nations Universal Declaration of Human Rights states that all people have an unqualified right to leave any country. Skilled migrants are not "owned" by their home countries, and should have the same rights to freedom of movement as professionals in rich countries.

Training Is Not A Waste of Money

The belief that skilled emigrants must cause public losses in the amount of their training cost is based on a series of stereotypes. First, large numbers of skilled emigrants are funded by themselves or by foreign scholarships. A survey of African-born members of the American Medical Association conducted by one of the authors found that about half of them acquired their medical training outside their country of birth. Second, many skilled emigrants serve the countries they come from for long periods before departure. The same survey found that African physicians in the United States and Canada who were trained in their country of birth spent, on average, over five years working in that country prior to emigration. This constitutes a substantial return on all investment in their training.

Skilled migrants are not "owned" by their home countries.

Third, there is the stereotype that skilled migrants send little money to their home countries, as they tend to come from elite families and bring their immediate families with them when they leave. But new research reveals this to be simply unfounded. Skilled migrants also tend to earn much more than unskilled migrants, and on balance this means that a university-educated migrant from a developing country sends *more* money home than an otherwise identical migrant with less education. The survey of African physicians mentioned above found that they typically send home much more money than it cost to train them, especially to the poorest countries. This means that for a typical African country as a whole, even if 100 percent of a physician's training was publicly funded, the emigration of that physician is still a net plus.

Fourth, it is simply not true that all higher education in low-income countries must take place under massive public subsidy. When publicly subsidized higher education is the only way for someone who is not already wealthy to acquire higher education, that person's emigration necessarily means that the subsidy emigrates too. But even in very low-income countries, there are alternative ways of financing higher education. One is to create ways for students to pay up front for their own training, as Makerere University in Uganda has done, but many African universities do not. Another is for the government to give students loans so that students can pay for their own training after the fact, which Kenya has done, but many African governments do not. Both of these break the necessary link between the departure of a worker and the departure of a public subsidy.

In the Philippines, training of the vast majority of nurses who leave the country is financed by the students themselves, the recruiters, or the foreign employers, not by the public; there is no reason whatsoever why similar professional schools could not be established throughout Africa.

The belief that skilled emigrants must cause public losses . . . is based on a series of stereotypes.

Many Migrants Return Home

A striking example comes from recent research in the Pacific, which has amongst the highest rates of skilled emigration globally. Consider Tonga, a small island nation with a population of only 100,000 where skilled workers might stereotypically be thought to have little incentive to go back. Even in this case, by age 35, just over a third of the nation's academic brightest who had migrated after high school were already back working in Tonga. And in Papua New Guinea, half of the most academically skilled migrants had returned home by their early 30s.

In the United States, more than 20 percent of foreign students receiving Ph.D.s already have firm commitments to return to their home countries at the time of graduation, and many more will likely return in subsequent years. Of course there is large variation across countries: Migrants are much more likely to return to booming economies with good job prospects, as is seen by the flows of Indian tech workers back to India in the last decade. But even in cases where few migrants return, those that do may be particularly motivated by a desire to help their home country and may return to key leadership positions. One recent calculation finds that since 1950, 46 current and 165 former heads of government received their higher education in the United States.

Allowing or encouraging doctors to leave Africa for rich destination countries can reduce the number of doctors within the countries they come from, although even this is not clear if more people undertake medical training with the hope of migrating. However, the level of medical care provided by doctors in Africa depends on a vast array of factors that have little or nothing to do with international movement—such as scant wages in the public health service, poor or absent rural service incentives, few other performance incentives of any kind, a lack of adequate medical supplies and pharmaceuticals, a mismatch between medical training and the health problems of the poorest, weak transportation infrastructure, or abysmal sanitation systems.

To illustrate just one of these—the lack of rural service incentives—policies that limit international movement choices per se do not change the strong incentive for African physicians to concentrate in urban areas far from the least served populations. Nairobi is home to just 8 percent of Kenya's population, but 66 percent of its physicians. More Mozambican physicians live in the capital Maputo (51 percent) than in the entire rest of Mozambique, though Maputo comprises just

8 percent of the national population. Roughly half of Ethiopian physicians work in the capital Addis Ababa, where only one in 20 Ethiopians lives.

This and the many other barriers to domestic effectiveness of physicians may explain why, across 53 African countries, there is no relationship whatsoever between the departure of physicians or nurses and poor health statistics as measured by indicators such as child mortality or the percentage of births attended by modern health professionals. If anything, the relationship is positive: African countries with the largest number of their physicians residing abroad in a rich country are typically those with the *lowest* child mortality, and vice versa. This suggests that whatever is determining whether or not African children live or die, other factors besides international migration of physicians are vastly more important. Fiddling with immigration or recruitment policies of destination countries do precisely nothing to address those underlying problems.

Overblown Hype

Just as fears about possible negative effects of brain drain are typically overblown, so is the hype over the ability of countries to tap their diaspora [expatriate population] to set up trade and investment. The well-known case of emigrants in Silicon Valley facilitating the growth of the Taiwanese, Chinese and Indian information technology industries is an important example demonstrating that high-skilled workers abroad can have transformative impacts on home country industry. But unfortunately, this is the exception rather than the rule.

In particular, skilled migrants from small islands and from sub-Saharan Africa, where highly skilled emigration rates are the highest, are not likely to be engaging in trade or investment. New surveys find that less than 5 percent of skilled migrants from Tonga, Micronesia and Ghana have ever helped a home country firm in a trade deal, and when they have, the amounts of such deals have been modest. Few migrants from these countries had made investments in their home countries—at most they had sent back amounts of US$2,000–3,000 to finance small enterprises.

"Brain drain" . . . would be best discarded in favor of a richer view of the links between human movement and development.

However, skilled workers do engage with their home countries in a number of other ways apart from remittances. They can be an important source of tourism for their home countries; more than 500,000 visitors to the Dominican Republic each year are Dominicans living abroad. They are also tourism promoters: 60–80 percent of skilled migrants from four Pacific countries and Ghana advise others about traveling to their home countries. They indirectly spur trade, through consuming their home country's products, and they transfer knowledge about study and work options abroad. The lack of involvement in trade and investment therefore largely reflects a lack of productive opportunities at home, not a lack of interest on the part of migrants in helping their home countries.

Conventional wisdom once held that the wealth of a country declined when it imported foreign goods, since obviously cash was wealth and obviously buying foreign goods sent cash abroad. [Scottish economist] Adam Smith argued that economic development—or the "wealth of nations"—depends not [on] a country's stock of cash but on structural changes that international exchange could encourage. In today's information age, the view has taken hold that human capital now rules the wealth of nations, and that its departure in any circumstance must harm a country's development. But economic development is much more complex than that.

But thanks to new research, we have learned that the international movement of educated people changes the incentives to acquire education, sends enormous quantities of money across borders, leads to movements back and forth, and can contribute to the spread of trade, investment, technology, and ideas. All of this fits very uncomfortably in a rhyming phrase like "brain drain," a caricature that would be best discarded in favor of a richer view of the links between human movement and development.

9

Americans Are Emigrating in Greater Numbers

Jay Tolson

Jay Tolson is a senior writer at U.S. News & World Report *and covers culture, ideas, and religion. He was previously the editor for the* Wilson Quarterly *and has contributed to many other publications, such as the* Washington Post *and* Slate.

A new trend in emigration is the number of Americans leaving the United States for better opportunities in foreign countries. Fed up with a failing economy and even worse politics, the largest number of these emigrants are entrepreneurs, teachers, skilled workers, and retirees. It is hard to estimate exactly how many are now living abroad because they are not counted in the U.S. census; however, some organizations have estimated the total to be between 4 million and 7 million.

Dressed in workout casual and sipping a soda in one of the apartment-style rooms of Los Cuatro Tulipanes Hotel, Matt Landau appears very much at home in Panama. One might even be tempted to call him an old hand were he not, at age 25, so confoundingly young. Part owner of this lovely boutique hotel in Panama City's historic Casco Viejo, he is also a travel writer (*99 Things to Do in Costa Rica*), a real estate marketing consultant, and editor of *The Panama Report*, an on-line news and opinion monthly. Between fielding occasional calls and text messages, the New Jersey native is explaining what drew him here, by way of Costa Rica, after he graduated from college in 2005. In addition to having great weather, pristine beaches, a rich melting-pot culture, a reliable infrastructure, and a clean-enough legal system, "what Panama is all about," he says, "is the chance to get into some kind of market first." Landau cites other attractions: "There is more room for error here," he says. "You can make mistakes without being put under. That, to me, as an entrepreneur, is the biggest draw."

Long a business and trade hub, Panama has been booming ever since the United States gave it full control of the Canal Zone in 1999. But as Landau says, it is precisely because so much of Panama's economy has been focused on canal-related activities that opportunities in other sectors, from real estate to finance to a host of basic services, have gone largely untapped. And among the many foreigners coming to tap them—as well as to enjoy the good life that Panama offers— are a sizable number of Americans.

These Yankees, it turns out, are part of a larger American phenomenon: a wave of native-born citizens who are going abroad in search of new challenges, opportunities, and more congenial ways of life.

In his recent book *Bad Money*, political commentator Kevin Phillips warns that an unprecedented number of citizens, fed up with failed politics and a souring economy, have already departed for other countries, with even larger numbers planning to do so soon. But that may be putting too negative a reading on this little-noticed trend. In fact, most of today's expats are not part of a new Lost Generation, moving to Paris or other European haunts to nurse their disillusionment and write their novels. Some may be artists and bohemians, but many more are entrepreneurs, teachers, or skilled knowledge workers in the globalized high-tech economy. Others are members of a retirement bulge that is stretching pensions and IRAs [individual retirement accounts] by living abroad. And while a high percentage of expats are unhappy with the rightward tilt of George Bush's America, most don't see their decision to move overseas as a political statement.

Southward trend. Europe still draws many of these American emigrants, but even more have relocated in Canada and Mexico. Others are trying out Australia, New Zealand, or one of the new economies of Asia, while a growing stream flows southward to Central and South America. John Wennersten, author of *Leaving America: The New Expatriate Generation* and a retired historian who has taught for many years abroad, says Panama is the "new new thing" for those who are part of what he calls "a long-term trend."

Exactly how many people are part of this trend is hard to say. Precise emigration figures have never been easy to come by in the United States. "It's been an implicit assumption that people come here to stay, not to come and go," says Mike Hoefer, head of the Office of Immigration Statistics at the Department of Homeland Security. The government's last trial effort to count Americans overseas, in 1999, was deemed inordinately expensive. Elizabeth Grieco, chief of immigration statistics at the U.S. Census Bureau, puts it bluntly: "We don't count U.S. citizens living abroad."

But if the government is not counting, others are. Estimates made by organizations such as the Association of Americans Resident Overseas put the number of nongovernment-employed Americans living abroad anywhere between 4 million and 7 million, a range whose low end is based loosely on the government's trial count in 1999. Focusing on households rather than individuals (and excluding households in which any member has been sent overseas either by the government or private companies), a series of recent Zogby polls commissioned by New Global Initiatives, a consulting firm, yielded surprising results: 1.6 million U.S. households had already determined to relocate abroad; an additional 1.8 million households were seriously considering such a move, while 7.7 million more were "somewhat seriously" contemplating it. If the data collected in the seven polls conducted between 2005 and 2007 are fairly representative of the current decade, then, by a modest estimate, at least 3 million U.S. citizens a year are venturing abroad. More interesting, the biggest number of relocating households is not those with people in or approaching retirement but those with adults ranging from 25 to 34 years old.

An unprecedented number of citizens, fed up with failed politics and a souring economy, have already departed for other countries.

According to Robert Adams, the CEO of New Global Initiatives, the motives of relocators are almost as hard to pin down as the numbers. "The only Americans who understand what's going on are those living abroad," he says. "There is no movement, no leader. It's just millions of people making individual decisions to do it."

Now living mostly in Panama City, Adams finds that the reasons people give for moving abroad often change, particularly among those who stay overseas for any length of time. In fact, he says, those who claim they came for a specific reason—for example, dissatisfaction with American politics—tend to be least happy with what they find in the new settings. By and large, most successful Americans abroad "are running *to* rather than running *from*," Adams stresses.

A new "West." Some observers even wonder whether words such as migration, emigration, and expatriation accurately describe most Americans' ventures abroad. Today, moving from the States to a place like Panama is almost tantamout to moving from the East Coast to the West Coast 50 years ago. And the Internet, Skype, and satellite television make it easy for people to stay in touch with the homeland. "While people are looking for something new, they're not giving up their citizenship," says Adams, who prefers the word relocation to emigration.

While American relocators are in some ways typical pioneers looking for a new "West," they are also participants in a larger, international development, "a global economic shift," Wennersten writes, "that is fostering real economic growth in heretofore-neglected areas of the world, like Latin America, Eastern Europe, and Southeast Asia." U.S. citizens are certainly not the sole beneficiaries of this shift, but they are active players in countries where the privatizing of former state-run industries and the opening of new capital and trade markets are creating an array of opportunities. "From computer consulting firms in Hong Kong to bagel shops in Budapest," Wennersten notes, "Americans are helping to revitalize or sustain economies that are receptive to Western entrepreneurship."

The motives of relocators are almost as hard to pin down as the numbers.

Talk to some of the successful American relocators around the world and the broad generalizations about them tend to hold up—though not so much as to overwhelm the huge variety of experience and achievement that distinguishes their lives. Michael Sheren, 45, who worked for Chemical Bank in New York in his early career, came to England in 1997 primarily to apply his background in leveraged buy-outs to the European market. Now working in the London office of Calyon Crédit Agricole, a French bank, he credits his American training and drive for giving him a leg up in his work. America's image abroad has suffered during the Bush years, he acknowledges, but he finds that Europeans still value the can-do spirit of Americans. "People equate America with success, even now," he says.

While business is what initially drew him to England, Sheren is now deeply attached to the British way of life. That includes everything from a generous government-backed system of social supports for all citizens to a mentality that is more comfortable with leisure. "I consider the quality of life here significantly better than what I would have over there," he says.

Sheren acquired British citizenship and has at times been tempted to abandon his American one, but he attaches relatively little importance to nationality. His closest friends are an international lot, and he greatly values the freedom of movement that comes with a European passport. "I feel more like a sovereign individual," he says, using the label coined by authors James Dale Davidson and William Rees-Mogg in their book, *The Sovereign Individual: Mastering the Transition to the Information Age.*

Talk to some of the successful American relocators around the world and the broad generalizations about them tend to hold up.

Immersion. Cynthia Barcomi, a Seattle-born artist, writer, and entrepreneur who came to Berlin in 1985 to launch her professional dancing career, stresses how different the expatriate life is from that of Americans who have been sent abroad by the government or private business. To her, it involves a much deeper immersion in the new culture. Like many of the relocators that Adams and Wennersten have dealt with, Barcomi says her motive for moving was more a deep hunch than a single, clearly articulated reason. She had seen a lot of German dance while a student at Columbia University, but she calls her final leap "a blind decision." She didn't even speak German.

After eight years with a professional dance troupe, Barcomi decided on another leap, this one into a new career as the founder and operator of what is now one of Berlin's most prominent coffee and baked goods stores. So successful did that venture prove that she later opened a deli under the Barcomi name. And between raising her children, she has written two respected cookbooks.

Barcomi's reflections on her expatriate life are nuanced: "I feel like the longer I live in Germany, the more I identify with being an American. It takes a while to realize how different we are from the Germans." But Barcomi also says that she has no intention of returning to the United States, even though she would never give up her passport. "I can't imagine living in the American rat race, even though I love America. I wouldn't leave here. I'm at the top of my game."

Like Sheren, Barcomi feels that her American attitudes and education, including her Girl Scout training, prepared her well for a successful life abroad. "I think perseverance is a distinctly American quality."

One big question is whether America is ultimately gaining or losing from this movement of bold, talented Americans into other countries. The answer is not simple. Wennersten cites what he estimates is a loss of about $30 billion in payroll, but he considers the outflow of expertise an even bigger potential drain. "It's not the average guys who are going," he says. "It's these 'creatives' who will be establishing the paradigm of the future."

Whether the relocation trend is heading toward a zero-sum outcome is something that you can't help pondering when you meet young American expatriates in Panama. If what they bring here in terms of skills, knowledge, and energy is Panama's gain, is America necessarily a loser?

Not if you look at what Jon Hurst is doing. Before starting the New York Bagel Café in the Cangrejo ("Crab") neighborhood of Panama City, the 38-year-old Arkansas native had spent a good part of his life helping others, from working with disabled adults in California to stints in the Peace Corps and the Crisis Corps in Central America. In fact, he sees the business he launched in 2006 as an extension of what he had recently been doing for an organization that focused on sustainable development in Panama and nearby countries. "One of the reasons I opened this place is to create a sustainable business that would help the local community," says Hurst.

One big question is whether America is ultimately gaining or losing from this movement of . . . Americans into other countries.

Coupling hard work with idealism, Hurst has built a store that has become a hub in this oldish, artsy quarter. His eight Panamanian employees are well paid and are learning about all aspects of the food business. The free WiFi and all-you-can-drink coffee, in addition to bagels and sandwiches, draw a lively mix of customers who conduct business, check their E-mail, or simply meet with friends. And while there are great challenges to life in Panama City, from appalling traffic to difficulty in getting equipment repairs, Hurst finds the Panamanians friendly and the local conditions (particularly the free trade zone and a modest regulatory regime) especially hospitable to small business. The Panamanian government encourages foreign entrepreneurs by giving microinvestor visas to those who put up at least $50,000 and employ at least three Panamanians. "I couldn't have opened this type of business in the States," says Hurst, who makes the same point that Landau does: "Here there's no one competing against me."

It may not be much of a stretch to say that today one of America's strongest exports is its skilled, energetic, and often idealistic relocators. If America's information-driven economy is the engine of globalization, it is fitting that Americans are working in those parts of the world that are being transformed by the process. They make up an entrepreneurial "peace corps"—establishing businesses, employing, instructing, setting examples, and often currying goodwill. It is a cliché, but still largely true, that many foreigners say that they distrust America but like Americans. These relocators have something to do with this.

And America itself is also learning something from those Americans abroad. "We're developing a breed of Americans who won't find it easy to go back home," says Adams, stating a truth that is not as negative as it sounds. Two Americans who exemplify that breed are Coley and Allison Hudgins, a couple with backgrounds in political and corporate consulting who now live in a small Pacific coast community about two hours from Panama City. She and a partner run a small short-term rental agency, while he and an associate head Latin American Venture Partners, locating investors for assorted building projects in the country.

Today one of America's strongest exports is its skilled, energetic, and often idealistic relocators.

Escaping "sameness." Doing most of their work out of their condo, the Hudginses have two young children whose education at a local Spanish-language Catholic school is supplemented with materials that their mother downloads from the Internet. Describing themselves as libertarians, the Hudginses went abroad out of discontent, not with American politics but with a dull sameness they found in American suburban life. Even though they did extensive planning for the move, they admit that the challenges of the new life are considerable. (Some of the greater ones are imposed by the U.S. government, which, though it grants an exemption of close to $86,000 of earnings, is the only developed nation that taxes citizens who are living abroad and paying foreign income taxes.) But both are quick to say that the rewards far outweigh the difficulties. In addition to valuing the warm weather, the idyllic setting, a close family life, and a busy social schedule, both are clearly invigorated by days that that are demanding but not stressful in a culture that blends the modern and the traditional in a comfortable way. They appreciate the irony that American know-how and technology (largely the Internet) make it possible for them to enjoy what is in many ways a very un-American lifestyle. But they are doubtful whether they can go home again. "We may decide to pack up and move on one day," Allison says. "But it's more likely that we'd find some new port of call than move back to the States."

Even if they don't return home, though, it is unlikely that what the Hudginses and other creative American relocators do will be lost on their compatriots back home. These relocators are part of a vast, generally benign cultural exchange, channeling different mores, attitudes, and ways of life back to America, even while bringing some distinctively American skills and attitudes to the wider world. Globalization may still seem like a grand abstraction, involving vast, impersonal forces, but the millions of Americans living and working abroad are part of its very human reality.

10

America Is Losing Skilled Workers Because of Immigration Laws

Vivek Wadhwa

Vivek Wadhwa is the Executive in Residence at Duke University's Pratt School of Engineering as well as a Wertheim Fellow at Harvard Law School's Labor and Worklife Program.

While many young foreigners choose to come to America to obtain their education and then find employment, our immigration and visa laws are making it nearly impossible to do so, forcing them to either return to their native countries or another country of their choosing. This causes the United States to lose highly skilled workers like engineers, scientists, and doctors after we have actually invested money in their educations. There has been an abundance of studies and research done on the impact that these laws are having on America and the numbers do not look good; however, the study on the contributions that these foreign students have made is the exact opposite, only proving that America is doing itself a disservice by not doing something about these laws.

From his early childhood, Sanjay Mavinkurve dreamed of coming to America and making it big. So his parents, who are from India, sent him to boarding school in Cleveland, Ohio when he was 14. He did so well that he gained a schol-

Vivek Wadhwa, "America's Other Immigration Crisis," *The American*, July/August 2008. Copyright © 2008 American Enterprise Institute for Public Policy Research. Reproduced with permission of The American Magazine, a national magazine of politics, business, and culture (www.american.com).

arship to Harvard, where he completed both a bachelor's and a master's degree in computer science. In his spare time, he helped conceive the design for Facebook and wrote its first computer code. After graduating, Sanjay joined Google and designed key parts of their mapping software for mobile devices.

Then Sanjay fell in love and had to choose between his heart and the American dream. He was in the United States on a temporary visa and was years away from obtaining permanent resident status. His fiancée had graduated from a top university in Singapore and started work as an investment banker. The only U.S. visa they could obtain for her would not allow her to work, and that would force her to abandon her ambitions. Instead, they decided to abandon America and move to Canada, which welcomed them with open arms.

The Problem with the H-1B Visa

The U.S. immigration system allows highly educated workers to enter the country for up to six years on a visa called the H-1B. But this visa imposes many restrictions. If these workers want to stay longer and enjoy the same rights as Americans, they need to obtain a permanent resident visa. And then after five years as a permanent resident, they can apply to become naturalized American citizens.

The problem is that there are more than a million skilled workers and their families in the United States who are waiting for these permanent resident visas, but there are hardly any visas available and the backlog is rapidly increasing. So, over the next few years, Sanjay's story is likely to be repeated many times.

These engineers, scientists, doctors, and researchers entered the country legally to study or to work. They contributed to U.S. economic growth and global competitiveness. Now we've set the stage for them to return to countries such as India and China, where the economies are booming and their skills are in great demand. U.S. businesses large and small stand to lose critical talent, and workers who have gained valuable experience and knowledge of American industry will become potential competitors.

My team at Duke University has been researching the impact of globalization on U.S. competitiveness and the sources of the U.S. advantage. We had many surprises in store when we looked at the role of immigrants in the tech sector.

What the Research Shows

In 1999, AnnaLee Saxenian of the University of California at Berkeley published a groundbreaking report on the economic contributions of skilled immigrants to California's economy. She found that Chinese and Indian engineers ran a growing share of Silicon Valley companies started during the 1980s and 1990s and that they were at the helm of 24 percent of the technology businesses started from 1980 to 1998. Saxenian concluded that foreign-born scientists and engineers were generating new jobs and wealth for the California economy.

We decided to update and expand her study and focus on engineering and technology firms started in the United States from 1995 to 2005. Over a period of two years, we surveyed thousands of companies and interviewed hundreds of company founders.

We found that the trend Saxenian documented had become a nationwide phenomenon. In over 25 percent of tech companies founded in the United States from 1995 to 2005, the chief executive or lead technologist was foreign-born. In 2005, these companies generated $52 billion in revenue and employed 450,000 workers. In some industries, such as semiconductors, the numbers were much higher—immigrants founded 35 percent of start-ups. In Silicon Valley, the percentage of immigrant-founded start-ups had increased to 52 percent.

When we looked into the backgrounds of these immigrant founders, we found that they tended to be highly educated—96 percent held bachelor's degrees and 74 percent held a graduate or postgraduate degree. And 75 percent of these degrees were in fields related to science, technology, engineering, and mathematics.

The vast majority of these company founders didn't come to the United States as entrepreneurs—52 percent came to study, 40 percent came to work, and 6 percent came for family reasons. Only 1.6 percent came to start companies in America. They found that the United States provided a fertile environment for entrepreneurship.

Even though these founders didn't come to the United States with the intent, they typically started their companies around 13 years after arriving in the country.

We uncovered some puzzling data in the World Intellectual Property Organization (WIPO) database, which is the starting point for obtaining information on global intellectual property protection. In 2006, foreign nationals residing in the United States were named as inventors or co-inventors in an astounding 26 percent of patent applications filed in the United States. This increased from 8 percent in 1998. Some U.S. corporations had foreign nationals contribute to a majority of their patent applications—such as Qualcomm at 72 percent, Merck at 65 percent, GE at 64 percent, and Cisco at 60 percent. Over 40 percent of the international patent applications filed by the U.S. government had foreign authors.

In 1998, 11 percent of these global patent applications had a Chinese inventor or co-inventor. By 2006 this percentage had increased to almost 17 percent. The contribution of Indians increased from 9 percent to 14 percent in the same period. To put these numbers into perspective, it is worth noting that Indians and Chinese both constitute less than 1 percent of the U.S. population, and census data show that 82 percent of Indian immigrants arrived in the United States after 1980.

But our concern was that these were foreign nationals and there was no certainty that they would stay and become U.S. citizens. These foreign-national inventors were also not from the same immigrant group that was founding high-tech companies—those were permanent residents or naturalized citizens. These inventors were likely to be Ph.D. researchers on student visas and employees of U.S. corporations on temporary visas like the H-1B, as Sanjay Mavinkurve was.

Immigrants . . . who file for permanent resident visas today could be waiting indefinitely.

The question was: Why was the number of foreign-national inventors increasing so dramatically—337 percent over 8 years?

To answer this, we had to develop our own methodology to estimate the population of skilled immigrants from which such inventors may originate.

We found that at the end of 2006, there were 200,000 employment-based principals waiting for labor certification, which is the first step in the U.S. immigration process. The number of pending I-140 applications, the second step of the immigration process, stood at 50,132. This was over seven times the number in 1996. The number of employment-based principals with approved I-140 applications and unfiled or pending I-485s, or the last step in the immigration process, was 309,823, a threefold increase from a decade earlier. Overall, there were 500,040 employment-based principals (in the three main employment visa categories of EB-1, EB-2, and EB-3) waiting for legal permanent residence. And the total including family members was 1,055,084.

These numbers are particularly troubling when you consider there are only around 120,000 visas available for skilled immigrants in the EB-1, EB-2, and EB-3 categories. To make things worse, no more than 7 percent of the visas are allocated to immigrants from any one country. So immigrants from countries with large populations like India and China have the same number of visas available (8,400) as those from Iceland and Poland.

Comprehending the Research

This means that immigrants like Sanjay who file for permanent resident visas today could be waiting indefinitely. H-1B visas are valid for up to six years and can be extended if the applicant has filed for a permanent resident visa. The problem is that once these workers have started the process, they can't change employers or even be promoted to a different job in the same company without taking the risk of having to restart the application process and move to the back of the line. Their spouses aren't allowed to work or obtain Social Security numbers, which are usually needed for things like bank accounts and driver's licenses. And these workers can't lay deep roots in American society because of the uncertainty about their future.

We also researched the trends in globalization and what was happening in India and China. We met dozens of executives of top companies in several industries in these countries and toured their R&D [research & development] labs.

In Hyderabad, India, companies like Satyam Computer Services and Hindustan Computers are designing navigation control and in-flight entertainment systems and other key components of jetliners for American and European corporations. In New Delhi, Indian scientists are discovering drugs for GlaxoSmithKline. In Pune, Indians are helping design bodies, dashboards, and power trains for Detroit automakers. In Bangalore, Cisco Systems, IBM, and other U.S. tech giants have made the Indian city their global base for developing new telecom solutions.

China is already the world's biggest exporter of computers, telecom equipment, and other high-tech electronics. Multinationals and government-backed companies are pouring hundreds of billions of dollars into next-generation plants to turn China into an export power in semiconductors, passenger cars, and specialty chemicals. China is lavishly subsidizing state-of-the-art labs in biochemistry, nanotech materials, computing, and aerospace.

Visit any of these labs, and you will meet dozens of workers returned from the United States—highly educated and skilled workers who received their education and training in top U.S. universities and corporations. In GE's Jack Welch Technology Center in Bangalore, 34 percent of the R&D staff have returned from the United States. So have 50 percent of those with a Ph.D. at IBM research in Bangalore. And so are the managers of China's top engineering, technology, and biotech companies.

These returnees have fueled much of the innovation and growth in R&D in China and India. And the executives of these companies will tell you that the number of résumés they receive from the United States has increased tenfold over the last few years.

Majority of Students Want to Stay

Most students and skilled temporary workers who come to the United States want to stay, as is evident from the backlog for permanent resident visas. Yet we're leaving these potential immigrants little choice but to return home. "The New Immigrant Survey," by Guillermina Jasso of New York University and other leading academics, found that approximately one in five new legal immigrants and about one in three employment principals either plan to leave the United States or are uncertain about remaining. These surveys were done in 2003, before the backlog increased so dramatically.

Additionally, there are over 250,000 foreign students studying in our universities. In our engineering schools, 60 percent of Ph.D. candidates and 42 percent of master's candidates are foreign nationals. These students are often the best of their home countries. But there are few visas available for U.S. companies to hire these students when they graduate. Foreign students can work temporarily when they graduate on practical training visas. But if they want to stay long term, they need to get H-1B visas and then file for permanent residence.

> *We have set the stage for hundreds of thousands of highly educated and skilled workers to become our competitors.*

The yearly allocation of H-1B visas for foreign students who graduate at the master's level and above is 20,000. But 31,200 people filed applications for these visas in the first week they became available in April of this year [2008]. Bachelor's-level graduates had even worse odds, as they had to compete in the general pool with only 65,000 visas available, less than half the number of applications for that visa category.

The result is that employers are now reluctant to hire foreign students. Why recruit and train new hires when there is less than a 50 percent chance that they will be able to stay? These students are getting increasingly frustrated and applying for jobs back home or in other countries.

So we have set the stage for hundreds of thousands of highly educated and skilled workers to become our competitors. Indian and Chinese industry benefited in a big way from the trickle of returnees over the last few years. Now we're looking at a flood.

Immigration Debate Focused on Wrong Issue

Immigration has been a hot topic in the media, but the focus has been on the plight of the estimated 12 million unskilled workers who entered the United States illegally. Emotions have been running high on the issues of amnesty and border control.

At the same time, a debate rages about H-1B visas and this gets considerable press coverage. Companies such as Microsoft, Intel, and Oracle have been lobbying for visas to bring in skilled immigrants, but have focused on expanding the numbers of H-1B visas available. Why? Perhaps because workers on these visas are desirable, as they are less likely to leave their employers during the decade or more they are waiting for permanent residence.

Employers are . . . reluctant to hire foreign students. Why recruit and train new hires when there is less than a 50 percent chance that they will be able to stay?

Moreover, I know from my experience as a tech CEO that H-1Bs are cheaper than domestic hires. Technically, these workers are supposed to be paid a "prevailing wage," but this mechanism is riddled with loopholes. In the tech world, salaries vary widely based on skill and competence. Yet the prevailing wage concept works on average salaries, so you can hire a superstar for the cost of an average worker. Add to this the inability of an H-1B employee to jump ship and you have a strong incentive to hire workers on these visas. (To be fair, the lobbying platform of these tech companies does include recommendations that the government expand the number of permanent resident visas.)

Opponents of H-1B visas complain that these visas cause job losses and damage the engineering profession. To some extent, they are right. If we bring in too many workers at the lower end of the scale, we could end up causing a reduction of salaries to the point that Americans don't consider the profession worthwhile. And there are indications that enrollments in computer science have already dropped. The fact is that if we flood the market with workers with any skill, we end up hurting individual members of the profession; if we brought in 100,000 doctors, dentists, or plumbers, we would cause salaries to drop, create unemployment, and discourage Americans from studying these professions.

The Problem Is Easy to Fix

So we want skilled immigrants, but we want them to come on the right visas as permanent residents. The battles being fought are about bringing in more people with H-1B visas—not about those who are already here with them and stranded in "immigration limbo." Which means that we're going to be compounding the hardship on workers who are already here and forcing more, like Sanjay, to abandon America.

We are now competing with the rest of the world for the best talent.

Unlike many of the problems facing the United States, this one isn't hard to fix. All we have to do is to increase the number of visas offered to skilled workers in the EB-1, EB-2, and EB-3 categories from 120,000 to around 300,000 per year. And we need to remove the per-country limits. Instead of requiring graduates from top universities who receive jobs from American corporations to go through the tedious H-1B visa process, we should provide a direct path to permanent residence. We are now competing with the rest of the world for the best talent. We need to do all we can to attract and keep skilled immigrants, rather than bring them here temporarily, train them, and send them home.

Organizations to Contact

The editors have compiled the following list of organizations concerned with the issues debated in this book. The descriptions are derived from materials provided by the organizations. All have publications or information available for interested readers. The list was compiled on the date of publication of the present volume: information provided here may change. Be aware that many organizations take several weeks or longer to respond to inquiries, so allow as much time as possible for the receipt of requested materials.

American Immigration Council (AIC)
1331 G St. NW, Suite 200, Washington, DC   20005
(202) 507-7500 • fax: (202) 742-5619
Web site: www.americanimmigrationcouncil.org

The AIC works to strengthen America by honoring the immigration system and encouraging the ethical treatment of immigrants, in turn influencing how America feels about immigration in the future. It focuses on educating Americans about the contributions and hard work of immigrants, standing up for fair immigration laws that reflect America's values and working hard for justice and fairness for immigrants according to the law. Its site offers information on education, policy, and laws in regard to immigration as well as current news articles.

American Immigration Lawyers Association (AILA)
1331 G St. NW, Suite 300, Washington, DC   20005
(202) 507-7600 • fax: (202) 783-7853
Web site: www.aila.org

AILA is a national association of immigration lawyers working toward fair immigration laws and policies, improving the quality of immigration and nationality law and practice as well as the professional development of its members. Not only does it work to improve the immigration laws and practices, but it also offers pro bono services to people in need of immigration law assistance. Its Web site offers access to many tools to assist the public in joining its cause, including its own online bookstore.

America's Voice

1050 Seventeenth St. NW, Suite 490, Washington, DC 20036
(202) 463-8602
Web site: www.americasvoiceonline.org

The goal of America's Voice is to offer education about the benefits of fair immigration reform that will honor legal immigration, reduce illegal immigration, maintain the importance of family reunification and respect the rights of all immigrants to fair and humane treatment. It reaches out to key audiences through the media, conducting public opinion research, communications, and online campaigns, as well as by offering its support to leaders who are taking a stand for immigration reform. The Web site offers facts on the different aspects of immigration as well as informative blogs.

Center for Immigration Studies

1522 K St. NW, Suite 820, Washington, DC 20005
(202) 466-8185 • fax: (202) 466-8076
e-mail: center@cis.org
Web site: www.cis.org

An independent, nonprofit research organization, the Center for Immigration Studies works to provide reliable information about the social, economic, and environmental consequences of immigration, legal and illegal, on the United States. Its Web site offers access to many different publications and videos as well as a book list for further reading.

Forced Migration Online (FMO)
Refugees Studies Centre, Oxford University
Oxford   OX1 3TB
   United Kingdom
fax: +44 1865-281801
e-mail: fmo@qeh.ox.ac.uk
Web site: www.forcedmigration.org

FMO is an online resource providing access to a wide range of relevant information on forced migration. Its main focus is to provide people with as much information on forced migration as is available, offering a digital library with downloadable files as well as a video library. It also offers a list of links to additional resources.

Globalization101.org
Levin Institute, New York, NY   10022
(212) 317-3566 • fax: (212) 521-5200
Web site: www.globalization101.org

Globalization101.org is an Internet resource started by the Levin Institute that aims to provide a better understanding of globalization. It provides information and interdisciplinary learning opportunities involving the controversy about globalization and the issues facing policy makers, including the changes in the international economy. The Web site contains a brief overview of the many different topics concerning globalization as well as a list of links to other helpful migration and globalization sites.

Immigration Voice
3561 Homestead Rd. #375, Santa Clara, CA   95051
(202) 386-6250 • fax: (202) 403-3853
e-mail: info@immigrationvoice.org
Web site: www.immigrationvoice.org

The goal of Immigration Voice is to organize resources and efforts in order to solve the many issues with the employment-based green card process, which is its current focus. It has recently enlisted the assistance of top public affairs firm Patton Boggs to aid in its fight. Its Web site offers a wealth of information on many topics pertaining to green card and visa issues.

International Organization for Migration (IOM)

1752 N St. NW, Suite 700, Washington, DC 20036
(202) 862-1826 • fax: (202) 862-1879
Web site: www.iom.int

The goals of the IOM are to ensure fair management of migration, encourage cooperation on migration issues, assist in finding solutions to migration problems and assist migrants in need, including refugees. Its main areas of focus are migration and development, facilitating and regulating migration, and forced migration. Its Web site offers a wealth of information, such as articles, personal stories, and statistics, as well as a video library.

Justice for Immigrants

United States Conference of Catholic Bishops
Washington, DC 20017
(202) 541-3174 • fax: (202) 722-8755
Web site: www.justiceforimmigrants.org

Justice for Immigrants' main goals are to educate the public on what the Catholic church teaches about migration, to encourage political leaders on positive immigration reform, and to assist qualified migrants in receiving the benefits of these reforms. To achieve its goals it is combining its efforts with the Catholic Campaign Against Global Poverty and reaching out to Catholic individuals and institutions nationally. The Web site offers a wealth of information on policies and how people can get involved, as well as current articles on the issue.

Lutheran Immigration and Refugee Service

700 Light St., Baltimore, MD 21230
(410) 230-2700 • fax: (410) 230-2890

e-mail: lirs@lirs.org
Web site: www.lirs.org

Lutheran Immigration and Refugee Service works with churches and organizations across the country to encourage cultural integration and financial self-sufficiency for families having to start over due to emigration. It aids in finding homes for orphaned migrant children and fights for legislation and policies that strengthen the rights of all immigrants, refugees, and their families. The Web site offers general information about its services as well as information about getting involved in the cause. It also includes a page with current news information regarding immigration and refugee issues.

Migration Information Source

Migration Policy Institute, Washington, DC   20036
(202) 266-1940 • fax: (202) 266-1900
Web site: www.migrationinformation.org

A project of the Migration Policy Institute, the Migration Information Source is an online resource that provides tools, data, and important facts on worldwide emigration. It employs a team of international correspondents to record global migration trends as well as offers different perspectives on the emigration debate. It gathers its information from a variety of sources, such as scholars on emigration and many global organizations and governments that make their information available on their site.

National Immigration Forum (NIF)

50 F St. NW, Suite 300, Washington, DC   20001
(202) 347-0040 • fax: (202) 347-0058
Web site: www.immigrationforum.org

NIF advocates for the value of immigration to the nation by using its communications, advocacy and policy expertise to develop strategies that lead to an America that treats all immigrants fairly. It focuses on campaigning for new legislation and laws as well as creating an understanding of all sides of the immigration issue, including those of the immigrant. Its Web site offers information on all facets of immigration as well as a link to contact one's local representative.

National Network for Immigrant and Refugee Rights (NNIRR)

310 Eighth St., Suite 303, Oakland, CA 94607
(510) 465-1984 • fax: (510) 465-1885
e-mail: nnirr@nnirr.org
Web site: www.nnirr.org

NNIRR is composed of local coalitions and immigrant, refugee, community, religious, civil rights, and labor organizations and activists creating a national forum to share information, educate communities and the general public, and develop solutions to immigration and refugee issues. It works to promote fair immigration and refugee policies in the United States as well as to defend and expand the rights of immigrants in the United States, no matter what their immigration status. Its Web site offers access to videos and publications, including its magazine *Network News*.

Negative Population Growth (NPG)

2861 Duke St., Suite 36, Alexandria, VA 22314
(703) 370-9510 • fax: (703) 370-9515
e-mail: npg@npg.org
Web site: www.npg.org

NPG is a national membership organization that works to educate American political leaders as well as the general public about the negative effects of overpopulation, due to immigration, on the environment and on overall quality of life. Through outreach and education programs, along with its media-campaigns, its goal is to mobilize Americans into demanding action against overpopulation. Its Web site offers links to its publications, such as *The NPG Journal*.

NumbersUSA

1601 N Kent St., Suite 1100, Arlington, VA   22209
(703) 816-8820
Web site: www.numbersusa.com

NumbersUSA was founded by author Roy Beck in response to the impact of immigration on United States communities, environment, and labor market. Its goal is to educate and motivate people to demand that lawmakers revise immigration laws. It provides resources such as statistics and graphs on the impact of immigration, videos, and up-to-date information on current immigration laws and issues.

Bibliography

Books

David Bacon — *Illegal People: How Globalization Creates Migration and Criminalizes Immigrants.* Boston: Beacon Press, 2009.

Jorge G. Castañeda — *Ex Mex: From Migrants to Immigrants.* New York: New Press, 2008.

Leo R. Chavez — *The Latino Threat: Constructing Immigrants, Citizens, and the Nation.* Palo Alto, CA: Stanford University Press, 2008.

Paul Collier — *The Bottom Billion: Why the Poorest Countries Are Failing and What Can Be Done About It.* New York: Oxford University Press, 2008.

Stephane Dufoix — *Diasporas.* Berkeley and Los Angeles: University of California Press, 2008.

Nancy L. Green and François Weil, eds. — *Citizenship and Those Who Leave: The Politics of Emigration and Expatriation.* Urbana: University of Illinois Press, 2007.

Rubén Hernández-León — *Metropolitan Migrants: The Migration of Urban Mexicans to the United States.* Berkeley and Los Angeles: University of California Press, 2008.

Tomás Jiménez — *Replenished Ethnicity: Mexican Americans, Immigration and Identity.* Berkeley and Los Angeles: University of California Press, 2009.

Kevin Johnson — *Opening the Floodgates: Why America Needs to Rethink Its Borders and Immigration Laws.* New York: New York University Press, 2009.

Russell King — *Atlas of Human Migration.* Richmond Hill, ON: Firefly Books, 2007.

Khalid Koser — *International Migration: A Very Short Introduction.* New York: Oxford University Press, 2007.

Mark Krikorian — *The New Case Against Immigration: Both Legal and Illegal.* New York: Sentinel HC, 2008.

Heather Mac Donald, Victor Davis Hanson, and Steven Malanga — *The Immigration Solution: A Better Plan than Today's.* Chicago: Ivan R. Dee, 2007.

Alejandro Portes and Rubén G. Rumbaut — *Immigrant America: A Portrait.* Berkeley and Los Angeles: University of California Press, 2006.

Michael Reid — *Forgotten Continent: The Battle for Latin America's Soul.* New Haven, CT: Yale University Press, 2009.

Daniel Sheehy — *Fighting Immigration Anarchy.* Bloomington, IN: iUniverse, 2009.

Apichai W. Shipper — *Fighting for Foreigners: Immigration and Its Impact on Japanese Democracy*. Ithaca, NY: Cornell University Press, 2008.

Peter Stalker — *The No-Nonsense Guide to International Migration*. Niagra Falls, NY: New Internationalist, 2008.

John R. Wennersten — *Leaving America: The New Expatriate Generation*. Santa Barbara, CA: ABC-CLIO, 2007.

Periodicals

Nabeela Ahmed — "What Donors May Learn from Emigrants' Remittances," *Devex*, September 24, 2008.

Alexei Bayer — "The New Emigration," *Moscow Times*, January 25, 2010.

Nina Bernstein — "A Fatal Ending for a Family Forced Apart by Immigration Law," *New York Times*, February 12, 2010.

Michael A. Clemens — "Let Them Leave," *Foreign Policy*, January 27, 2010.

Sam Dolnick — "Myanmar's Frustrated Generation Looks Abroad," *America's Intelligence Wire*, July 5, 2009.

Economist — "Hot, Dry and Crowded," February 6, 2010.

Economist — "Migration: Open Up," January 3, 2008.

Barry Hatton   "Portuguese Rely on Survival Strategies amid Slump," *America's Intelligence Wire*, June 16, 2009.

Joshua Hoyt   "Get Off the Fence," *U.S. Catholic*, February 2010.

Carolyn Lochhead "Conflict in Iraq/Iraq Refugee Crisis Exploding," *San Francisco Chronicle*, January 16, 2007.

Prakash Naidoo   "Skills Shortage: Engineering Trouble," *Financial Mail* (South Africa), June 19, 2009.

Louis Nevaer   "Many Americans Moving to Mexico in Search of the American Dream," *New America Media*, March 30, 2009.

Michael Petrou   "Europe's War Against Islam," *Maclean's*, January 18, 2010.

Julia Preston   "Mexican Data Show Migration to US Decline," *New York Times*, May 14, 2009.

Peter Schaeffer   "Refugees: On the Economics of Political Migration," *International Migration*, February 2010.

Adriana Stuijt   "Young Whites Emigrate, Young Blacks Die of TB-AIDS in S. Africa," *Digital Journal*, November 27, 2008.

Marisa Treviño   "The Flipside of the Immigration Issue: American Emigrants Impact Mexico," *Latina Lista*, January 14, 2008.

Hendrick P. Van Dalen and Kene Henkens	"Longing for the Good Life: Understanding Emigration from a High-Income Country," *Population and Development Review*, March 1, 2007.
Lindsay Wagner	"The Psychological Effects of Emigrating," *Buzzle*, April 17, 2008. www.buzzle.com.
Allan Wall	"Memo from Mexico," *VDare.com*, February 16, 2006. www.vdare.com.
Allan Wall	"Mexican Emigration Versus Economic Development," *Banderas News*, June 2007. www.banderasnews.com.
Danny Westneat	"Not Enough to Make Him Stay," *Seattle Times*, November 9, 2006.

Index